Personal Finance Essentials

How to Track Expenses, Avoid Fraud, and Build a Sustainable Financial Future

Oliver J. Sage

Resilient Life Publishing

Other Books by Oliver J. Sage

Practical guides to money, investing, and the systems that shape modern financial life.

Crypto Made Simple for Seniors

A clear, jargon-free introduction to cryptocurrency: how it works, how to use it safely, and how to avoid the mistakes that cost people money.

Personal Finance Essentials

A practical system for understanding where your money goes, reducing unnecessary expenses, and building a stable financial foundation that holds over time.

The Age of Influence

A grounded look at how influence, media, and online platforms shape what we buy, believe, and trust: and how to think clearly within it.

ISBN 978-1-7638911-0-4

Thanks to

Fran and Family

for your support, and

for keeping me grounded.

Contents

Start Here

Let's talk about that moment when something doesn't add up.

A bill arrives you weren't expecting. A payment date creeps up faster than it should. You check your account and feel it immediately, that quiet, sinking realization that things are tighter than they should be.

It rarely happens all at once. It builds. Small gaps. Shortfalls. One decision layered on top of another. Before long, money is moving, but nothing seems to stay.

Living week to week becomes normal. Balances hover near their limits. One expense replaces another, and the space to think clearly about any of it disappears.

I've been there.

Not in theory, but in practice. After a series of hits, divorce, unexpected costs, things breaking when they couldn't afford to, the margin disappeared. What was left was pressure, decisions made too quickly, and a growing sense that things were slipping out of control.

Getting out of that position didn't come from a single fix. It came from understanding what was actually happening, making adjustments, and building something more stable, step by step.

That's what this book is for.

Not theory. Not quick wins. A system.

We're going to work through three parts:

First, understanding where your money is actually going, not where you think it's going.

Second, tightening the leaks, the small, repeated decisions that quietly drain your income.

Third, building a structure that holds, something sustainable, not something that works for a week and collapses.

None of this is complicated. But it does require attention and honesty.

If you work through it properly, not perfectly, just consistently, things begin to change. Slowly at first, then more noticeably.

This is where that shift starts.

This isn't a theory book.

Throughout the chapters, you'll find practical examples, simple frameworks, and short tips you can apply straight away.

You don't need to do everything at once. Work through what's relevant, apply what makes sense, and come back to the rest when you need it.

Some sections will be more reflective, others more practical. That's intentional. Understanding and action work together.

Chapter One

Assessing Your Financial Situation

You can only improve that which you have measured.

The first step is understanding where you actually stand.

Look at your income, your expenses, your debt, and your savings. Not roughly, properly.

Once you see the full picture, it becomes much easier to spot where things need to change. That's the foundation everything else is built on.

In this chapter, we'll walk through how to assess your financial position, track your spending, and recognise the patterns that are shaping your situation.

From there, you can begin setting clear short-term and long-term financial goals.

Evaluating Your Current Financial Health

Your financial health is comprised of several components: income, expenses, debt, and assets.

Here's a step-by-step guide to evaluate your current financial situation:

Income:

Begin by identifying all your income sources. This includes:

Primary income: Your salary or hourly wages from your full-time job. It's your net income (after taxes) that truly matters when building a budget.

Side hustles: If you have side gigs, freelance work, or any additional jobs, include the income from these sources.

These are often less consistent, so average what you've earned over the past several months to get a realistic figure.

Passive income: If you earn money from investments, rental properties, dividends, or royalties, include these as part of your total income.

Take the average of these if they are infrequent payments. Passive income can be a powerful tool for building long-term wealth.

Other sources: Any other income, such as government benefits, child support, or financial assistance, should also be included.

Once you've listed all your income sources, total them to get your monthly income. This figure will be the basis for your budget.

Outgoings or Expenses:

Now to understand where your money goes each month. This is as important as knowing how much you make. Outgoings are generally categorized as either fixed or variable:

Fixed expenses are predictable costs that remain constant from month to month.

Typically, these are rent or mortgage payments, insurance premiums, student loans, personal loans, and car payments. Your budget must prioritize these expenses.

Variable expenses: These fluctuate from month to month and include utilities, groceries, transportation (fuel or public transit), dining out, entertainment, shopping, and discretionary spending.

Unlike fixed expenses, there's more flexibility in how much you spend in these areas.

Credit cards: Your minimum monthly payments must also be accounted for.

These tend to be high-interest debt and can quickly become a financial burden.

PayPal Pay as You Go and Similar: These are short-term debits that help spread a single payment over a couple of months.

They will be directly debited from your credit card so you need to allow for them.

Buy Now and Pay Later: This is not free money. These are loans that allow the store to sell you a product, and they get the cash from the Service Provider; you get the goods now, and the payment is deferred until later.

This can be a lifesaver when your major appliance blows up and you simply cannot find the cash or credit to pay for a replacement outright. There is a major caveat here, though. If you do not pay them off before the "Pay Later" date arrives, then they normally convert to a very high-interest-rate debt that needs to be paid down.

Bridging finance; You may have taken a Bridge Loan to assist you buy a new property while you await the sale of your existing residence.

These loans are short-term in nature and are also seen as a higher risk to the provider, so they carry a higher interest rate than mortgages.

You need to factor in the monthly interest and deduct the loan payout from the settlement of your property sale to finalise the loan.

Knowing how much you pay each month toward debt helps determine how much of your income is consumed by debt servicing.

We will look deeper at tracking your expenses. Still, it requires gathering receipts, reviewing bank statements, and/or using a mobile app that automatically categorizes and records spending.

Completing this step will give you a clearer picture of where you're overspending and where you can adjust accordingly.

Debt Assessment:

Debt, and how to pay it off, is the most stressful aspect of personal finance. To gain control over your debt, you need to know:

Total debt balance: Write down the total amount owed on all loans and credit cards. Be honest about your situation, facing the complete picture is better than underestimating.

Interest rates: Different debts carry different interest rates and can be categorized as:

1. High-interest debts, like credit card balances and short-term loans,
2. Medium Interest rates, like personal or car loans
3. Lower Interest rates, such as mortgages and student loans.
4. Unless you have a fixed-rate mortgage (which possibly only lasts for a set number of years), the lender can and will periodically adjust the rate, and you will need to account for any changes.

Prioritizing which debts to pay off first (usually starting with the highest interest rate) can lead to significant savings over time.

You might also explore debt consolidation or refinancing options to reduce your overall interest payments. We will talk about this further in Chapter 2.

Assets:

Your financial health isn't just about what you owe, it's also about what you own. Assets include:

Cash savings: How much do you have in your bank accounts?

Investments: This includes any stocks and shares, bonds, retirement accounts (like a 401(k), IRA, or superannuation), Crypto, precious metals, and other investments.

Property: If you own real estate (the equity after subtracting any mortgages or liens against it), vehicles (the depreciated value), or other valuable assets, include these in your assessment.

Your net worth is the difference between your assets and liabilities (debts). This number gives you an overall snapshot of your financial health.

It can be a powerful motivator for improving your situation.

Tracking Expenses

Tracking your expenses is one of the most effective ways to take control of your financial situation. Many people are surprised when they realize how much money they spend on unnecessary items.

The key to managing your expenses is to track them carefully and consistently.

Manual Tracking: The traditional method of writing down every transaction in a notebook or spreadsheet.

This method forces you to be aware of each dollar you spend, which is a powerful psychological tool for curbing unnecessary purchases.

Spreadsheets: Using a simple spreadsheet allows you to categorize your expenses and gives you a lot of flexibility to set up your own requirements.

It is the most secure, as you are not sharing your financial details or plans with anyone else.

Using Apps: If manual tracking isn't your style, plenty of digital tools are available on the Internet to help you automate the process.

Some can link to your bank and credit accounts to automatically track your transactions. I suggest contacting your bank to find out what apps they recommend and whether they own them. If they do own them, that is a much more secure way of ensuring the security of your information and accounts.

I would not recommend going with any third-party apps because no matter what promises they may make upfront, there is little you can do if they on-sell the app.

Bank owned apps are probably going to be free or have a minimal cost to you, as they are creating these apps as a service to their customers to keep their custom, whereas third-party apps will have monthly or yearly fees attached to them.

Be Diligent and Honest: Whether you use manual tracking or apps, consistency and honesty are essential.

Include every expense, no matter how small, to get an accurate picture of your spending habits. Small transactions, like morning coffees or snacks, might seem insignificant, but they can add up over time.

By tracking your expenses carefully, you'll gain control over your spending and find areas where you can save.

Identifying Spending Patterns

After tracking your expenses for a few weeks, patterns will emerge. Identifying these patterns is crucial for controlling your finances and adjusting your spending habits.

Common Spending Pitfalls: Most people have spending habits that they don't even realize. Here are some common patterns:

1. **Emotional spending**: Do you tend to spend more when stressed, tired, or bored? Emotional spending can be a significant drain on your budget, especially if you find yourself shopping for things you don't need as a way to cope with negative emotions.

2. **Impulse purchases**: Many people make impulsive purchases—especially in today's world of one-click online shopping.

Lifestyle creep: As your income increases, you will probably find that your spending also increases. While this is quite natural, unchecked lifestyle creep can prevent you from reaching your financial goals.

Analyze Your Spending Categories: Once you've tracked your spending, categorize and review each category. For example:

1. **Housing and utilities**: Are you spending more than 30% of your income on rent or mortgage? If so, consider more affordable housing if it is available.

2. **Groceries**: Are you sticking to a grocery budget or making frequent trips for non-essential items?

3. **Entertainment**: How much of your monthly budget goes toward discretionary entertainment? Could you find free or low-cost alternatives to your favorite activities?

Plugging Money Leaks: Money leaks are small, often unnoticed expenses that add up over time. Some examples include:

1. **Subscription services** include streaming platforms, meal kits, software licenses, and other subscriptions you don't use regularly but continue paying for.
2. **ATM fees**: Frequent ATM withdrawals can result in high bank fees, which could be avoided by fore-planning and using bank-affiliated ATMs.
3. **Credit card interest**: Carrying a balance on your credit cards leads to high interest charges. Paying down these balances can save you significant money in the long run.

By identifying spending patterns, you will see areas where you can reduce or eliminate unnecessary expenses and focus on saving more.

Setting Financial Goals: Short-Term and Long-Term

Having clear goals will give you the motivation and direction to manage your money better and enable you to build a better financial future.

Short-Term Financial Goals: Short-term goals are typically achievable within a year or less.

These goals help you focus on immediate improvements to your financial situation. Examples include:

1. **Building an emergency fund**: This should be a top priority if you do not have one. Start by setting a goal to save at least $1,000, then work towards saving six months of living expenses.
2. **Paying off high-interest debt**: Prioritize paying down debts with the highest interest rates, such as credit card debt. Set a goal to pay off a specific amount of debt within a set timeframe, such as reducing your credit card balance by $2,000

in the next six months.

Creating a budget: If you're new to budgeting, a short-term goal might be sticking to a written budget for the next three months.

Long-Term Financial Goals: Long-term goals take more time to achieve and usually require more planning and dedication. Examples include:

1. **Saving for retirement**: Retirement may feel far away, but the earlier you start saving, the more your money can grow through compound interest. Set a goal to contribute a certain percentage of your income to retirement accounts.

2. **Saving for a major purchase**: Whether saving for a home down payment, a car, or a dream vacation, set a specific savings goal and break it down into monthly contributions.

3. **Becoming debt-free**: Eliminating all debt can take years, but setting small, incremental goals (such as paying off one debt at a time) can help you stay motivated.

Setting SMART Goals: To make your goals effective, use the SMART framework:

1. **Specific**: Clearly define your goal. Instead of saying, "I want to save more," say, "I will save $500 per month for the next 12 months."

2. **Measurable**: Make sure your goal is measurable. You can measure monthly progress in the example above to ensure you're on track.

3. **Achievable**: Set realistic goals based on your current financial situation. Only aim to save $5,000 in a month if your income supports it.

4. **Relevant**: Ensure your goals align with your long-term vision. If becoming debt-free is your priority, focus your short-term goals on debt repayment.

5. **Time-bound**: Assign a deadline to your goal, which will create urgency and help you stay focused.

Breaking Down Long-Term Goals: Long-term goals can feel overwhelming if you look at them as a whole.

- Example: Saving $50,000 for a house down payment might seem impossible. However, it becomes more achievable by breaking that goal into smaller, manageable steps (saving $525 per month for 8 years).

Setting short- and long-term goals gives you a clear roadmap for your financial journey.

These goals will keep you motivated and help you stay on track as you work toward financial security.

Chapter Two

Reducing Monthly Expenses

A dollar saved today is a dollar for tomorrow.

Most people don't realise how much money slips away each month.

Not through big decisions, but through small, repeated habits that go unnoticed.

This chapter is about finding those gaps, and closing them.

By reducing your monthly expenses, you not only save but regain control of your finances. This allows you to do things that you don't even see as possibilities right now. In this chapter, we'll uncover practical strategies to cut: housing, transportation, food, entertainment, and debt repayment costs, without sacrificing your quality of life.

Get ready to take the first step toward building the life you've always envisioned.

Saving on Housing and Utilities

Housing is often the single most significant monthly expense. Still, there are several ways to lower this cost, even if moving is not an option.

Let's explore strategies to save on housing and reduce utility bills.

Downsizing Your Living Space: Think about your current residence, is it too large or too expensive for your needs? Could changes lead to substantial savings? Moving into a smaller apartment, renting out a room, or finding a roommate can significantly reduce your rent or mortgage payments. Downsizing lowers your monthly housing costs and decreases expenses like utilities, home maintenance, and even furniture.

- **Example**: We had a big house on a large plot of land in a sought-after suburb. After a series of interest rate hikes, our mortgage repayments, along with the regular maintenance, were killing us. We sold up and purchased a smaller house in a good but not-so-exclusive suburb with a much smaller mortgage.
- Not only did we save on the mortgage repayments, but we also had less work to do to maintain the place.
- As it was significantly smaller, our utilities were reduced along with the city taxes.

A Word of Caution: Perhaps your present home is in a free public transportation zone, or you can and do walk or cycle to work. Moving much further from this location can severely impact your outgoings because of the increased transport costs. If you own the home, you could also find that you do not achieve the same rate of capital growth, which could be quite a significant factor long term.

Pros and Cons: As with every major decision, you need to sit down and make a list of the pros and cons of this. Factor in access to amenities. If you have children, school zones, and quality of teaching. If selling, agents fees, and any taxes or refinancing costs. If renting, any letting fees, bond, or deposit requirements. The cost of moving your household items.

All this will give you a clearer understanding of what it is all going to cost and whether it is actually better to just stay where you are and try some of the other methods I will describe, to make the savings that you want to achieve.

Negotiating Rent: If you're renting, you can consider re-negotiating for a lower rent from your landlord when your lease is about to expire. Many landlords prefer to keep good tenants rather than go through the hassle and cost of finding new ones. There may be room to negotiate a lower rate, especially if you are able to show that the average rents in your area are lower than what you are paying.

Sometimes, offering extra rent upfront or even signing for a longer lease can make all the difference in these negotiations.

Refinancing Your Mortgage: Homeowners with mortgages can often save by refinancing to a lower interest rate. Even slightly reducing this will result in monthly savings and reduce the total amount you'll pay over the life of the loan.

It is crucial to weigh the costs of refinancing (such as closing fees, establishment fees, etc.) against the potential savings because it might not be worth it.

Bear in mind, though, that these types of loans have very long lifespans, so these costs are amortized over this long period. So, although they may be significant, if you are planning to remain in the same place for a long period, they may not be such a factor. Alternatively, if you can see yourself moving in a year or two, then it may not make a lot of sense to refinance now.

Cutting Utility Costs: Utilities like electricity, water, and heating are a significant portion of your monthly expenses. The following are ways to reduce these costs:

1. **Energy-efficient appliances**: As a renter, you could consider changing to LED light bulbs and making sure you turn off appliances when not in use. If you own your own home, you can look to install energy-efficient appliances, etc. These appliances will be a significant outlay, but they can pay for themselves over time.

2. **Programmable thermostats**: Installing a programmable thermostat will save money on utility bills by automatically adjusting the temperature when you're not at home or while you are sleeping.

3. **Insulate your home**: Proper insulation can reduce heating and cooling costs by retaining heat in winter and keeping the interior cooler in summer.

4. **Water-saving fixtures**: Installing low-flow shower-heads and faucets will help reduce your water bill without compromising comfort and come with a minimal cost, especially if you DIY the fitting.

Cutting the Cord on Cable: are you still paying for traditional cable packages when more affordable options are available? Streaming services such as Netflix, Hulu, BritBox, and Amazon Prime Video offer more flexibility and often cost a fraction of the price.

Think about how much TV you watch and consider cancelling your cable subscription for more affordable alternatives.

Switching to a Cheaper Internet Plan: Many people pay for high-speed Internet plans they don't need. If you're not a heavy gamer or don't frequently stream 4K video, a lower-tier plan could meet your needs at a much lower cost.

Additionally, some internet providers offer discounted rates if you bundle services, such as adding your mobile phone to your ISP plan, or agree to a longer contract.

Shop around and compare the various ISP's offerings.

Lowering Transportation Costs

Transportation is another significant expense, but there are several ways to reduce these costs, whether you own a car or rely on public transportation.

Carpooling and Ride-sharing: Sharing rides with others can drastically reduce fuel and vehicle maintenance costs. Platforms like Waze Carpool, UberPool, and Lyft Shared allow you to share rides with people heading in the same direction, splitting the cost of fuel and tolls. you could also consider organizing a carpool with coworkers or neighbors for regular commutes to work or school.

Switching to Public Transportation: Public transportation is significantly cheaper than driving in many cities. Monthly passes for buses, trains, or subways can save you hundreds of dollars yearly on gas, parking, and maintenance costs and, at the same time, are cheaper than purchasing multiple single-use tickets.

Even if public transportation isn't an option for your daily commute, consider using it for occasional trips to the city or social events to avoid paying for parking and gas.

Think About Biking or Walking: If you live in a bike-friendly area, investing in a good-quality bike can pay off in the long run, especially if it replaces a significant portion of your driving. The bonus is that the extra exercise you get from biking or walking is not only saving you money but improving your health.

Refinance Your Auto Loan: If you have a car loan with a high interest rate, refinancing the loan can lower your monthly payments. Make sure to shop around for better rates and terms and use a loan calculator to see how much you'll save over the life of the loan.

Shop for Cheaper Car Insurance: Insurance premiums can vary widely between providers. Compare quotes from multiple insurance companies at least once a year to ensure you get the best deal. Before you do this, spend a little bit of time checking the selling price of similar vehicles with similar condition and mileage.

You can also ask your current provider about discounts for bundling insurance policies, having a safe driving record, or installing anti-theft devices.

Some Car insurance companies also offer discounts to their policies based on the usage of the vehicle. An example would be if you use your vehicle less than a fixed mileage per year. You provide the odometer reading at the start and end of the year, but if you exceed the fixed amount it usually means any claim would result in a higher excess.

However, these types of policy can save significant amounts.

- **Example**: Reviewing the insurance on one of our vehicles showed that the insured value was $13,000 dollars, but all the similar cars I found on dealers' sites, with similar mileage, were worth only $8,000 dollars. I then got 2 quotes from different companies and saved just over $500 per year.
- I also saw that the insurance was for replacement value and not an agreed value. So, if the vehicle were written off in an accident, I would have only gotten the $8000 dollars replacement value. Even though the premium was being calculated on the $13000.

Food and Grocery Shopping on a Budget

Food is a necessity, but many people overspend without realizing it. A more strategic approach to grocery shopping and meal planning can significantly reduce food costs.

Meal Planning: Pre-planning your meals is one of the most effective ways to save money on groceries. It helps you avoid impulse buys and cuts down on food waste. Choose a day each week to plan out your meals and create a shopping list based on the ingredients you'll need.

Stick to this list when grocery shopping to avoid buying unnecessary items.

Buy in Bulk: Purchasing items such as grains, pasta, canned goods, and household essentials in bulk can save you money in the long run.

Stores like Costco, Sam's Club, and BJ's Wholesale offer significant discounts for bulk purchases.

Shop at Discount Grocery Stores: Many stores, such as Costco, Aldi, or Lidl, offer the same products as traditional supermarkets but at a fraction of the cost.

These stores focus on private-label brands, which are often of comparable quality to name brands but much cheaper.

Use Coupons and Cashback Apps: Digital coupons and cashback apps can help you save money on groceries.

Apps like Ibotta, Fetch Rewards, and Rakuten offer cashback on groceries. At the same time, websites like Coupons.com allow you to find digital or printable coupons.

Many grocery stores also have loyalty programs offering discounts or rewards for frequent shopping.

Shop Store Brands: These are often as good as major brands without the higher cost. Items like pasta, cereal, canned goods, and cleaning supplies are great candidates for switching to store brands. Over time, these small savings can add up to significant amounts.

Cut Down on Dining Out: Eating out is one of the easiest ways to overspend on food. While dining out can be enjoyable, cooking at home can be much less expensive. Limit dining out to special occasions or set a monthly budget for restaurant meals.

Cooking at home saves money and gives you control over the ingredients and portion sizes.

- **Tip**: Prepare meals in bulk and refrigerate or freeze leftovers for later use. This will ensure that you have future meals available and reduce the temptation to order takeout on busy nights. The added bonus is that you will reduce food waste and garbage disposal while saving money.

Grow Your Own Food: If you have space for a garden, growing your own fruits, vegetables, and herbs can save you money on produce.

Even if you live in a small apartment, container gardening or windowsill herb gardens can provide you with fresh ingredients at a fraction of the cost.

Entertainment and Lifestyle Choices

Entertainment is a significant area where many people overspend, but it doesn't have to be expensive to have fun. You can still enjoy a rich social life without blowing your budget by making a few adjustments.

Opt for Free or Low-Cost Entertainment: There are countless free or low-cost entertainment options, from community events and outdoor concerts to movie nights at home. Many cities offer free or donation-based events such as outdoor yoga classes, art shows, or film screenings.

- **Tip**: Check your local library for free entertainment resources. Many libraries offer free movie rentals, digital book loans, and passes to local museums and attractions.

Cut Back on Subscriptions: Subscription services, such as streaming platforms, magazines, software licenses, and gym memberships, can quietly eat away at your budget if you're not careful. Review all your subscriptions and cancel the ones you don't use regularly.

Consider switching to free or cheaper alternatives when possible.

Host Social Gatherings at Home: Instead of going out to restaurants or bars with friends, host a potluck or game night. This way, you can enjoy socializing without the high cost of dining out or paying for drinks. You can even make it a themed event, such as a movie marathon or a cooking competition, to make it more fun.

Find Discounted Tickets: For concerts, shows, or sporting events, look for discounted tickets on websites like StubHub, Goldstar, or Groupon. Many venues also offer last-minute discounts or promotions for students and seniors.

Reducing Debt-Related Expenses

Debt can be a heavy financial burden, but there are ways to reduce the costs of managing it. By minimizing interest payments and avoiding fees, you can focus on paying off your debts faster and saving money.

Debt Consolidation: If you have multiple debts with high interest rates, consolidating them into a single loan with a lower interest rate can save you money. Debt consolidation loans or balance transfer credit cards with low introductory rates are great options for simplifying your payments and reducing interest. Just be sure to avoid adding new debt during the process.

- **Example**: Say you have three credit cards with interest rates of 18%, 22%, and 25%. If you consolidate them into one loan with a 10% interest rate, you will cut your interest payments by more than half. Having only the one loan will also make it easier to focus on paying it down.

Negotiate Lower Interest Rates: Many people don't realize you can negotiate with your credit card company, or lender, to lower your interest rate. If you've been a responsible borrower, call your credit card issuer and ask for a lower rate. Even a reduction of just a few percentage points can significantly affect how much you pay in interest over time.

If your lender is not amenable, look for another that will roll over your debt into a lower fees and interest instrument.

Refinance Loans: Refinancing student loans, car loans, or mortgages can result in lower interest rates and monthly payments. Refinancing can make sense if you can secure a lower interest rate than your current loan and if the fees associated with refinancing don't outweigh the savings.

Set Up Automatic Payments: Setting up automatic payments for your credit cards or loans ensures that you never miss a payment and incur late fees. Many lenders also offer small interest rate reductions for enrolling in automatic payments, so it's worth asking your provider if this is an option.

As you can see there are a lot of ways to reduce monthly expenses, and as you start to use them then I am sure you will become even more inventive and come up with some of your own.

The biggest thing is that this has made you aware that you always have options.

How you exercise that knowledge is up to you but just knowing this will begin to reflect in your life from now on.

Chapter Three

Financial Discipline and Mindset

Mastering your mindset is the key to unlocking your full financial potential, start with belief, and the rest will follow

Discipline matters, but mindset is what holds it together.

You can have the best plan in the world, but if your thinking doesn't support it, it won't last. Temptation, stress, and impulsive decisions have a way of undoing even the most carefully set budget.

This chapter looks at what's really going on behind spending and saving, why we make the choices we do, and how to bring a bit more control to them.

We'll cover how to build delayed gratification, stay consistent when things get difficult, and develop a mindset that actually supports the financial changes you're trying to make.

Crafting Your Personal Financial Vision

Before we get into the detail it is very helpful to create a clear financial vision that provides motivation and direction in financial planning. It will serve as a guidepost for decision-making and help you stay committed to your financial goals.

Start by visualizing your ideal financial future, whether it's being debt-free, owning a home, or retiring early. Use vision boards, journaling, or visualization exercises to solidify your aspirations. Defining short-term and long-term financial goals using the SMART

(Specific, Measurable, Achievable, Relevant, and Time-bound) framework helps create structured plans for achieving financial success.

- **Example**: John has managed to accrue a debt of 15000 dollars on his credit cards.
- After doing his budget he realises that by cutting back on his incidental expenses he can afford to allocate 700 dollars a month to clear the debt.
- By setting up his automatic payment so the money is drawn down the day after his fortnightly pay going into his account, he will have the card paid down in 3.5 years.
- To give him additional motivation he draws up a timeline of payments and attaches it to the fridge door.
- Each fortnight he crosses off the payment and he is positively reminded of his progress every time he goes to the fridge.

This is a simple example of one part of Johns vision, He can expand this to include longer term goals of saving to be able to have a down payment to buy a house, take a year off for travel in the future, or any other life goals he might envision.

Aligning your financial plans with personal values ensures that your financial goals reflect what truly matters to you. Crafting a financial mission statement, a concise declaration of your financial aspirations, can serve as a daily reminder of your goals and motivate you to make disciplined financial choices.

The Psychology of Spending and Saving

Understanding the psychology behind why we spend money can help you take control of your financial behavior.

Many of our spending habits are not rational but emotional, so let's explore some of the triggers that influence how we spend and how to combat them.

Emotional Spending: Many people shop to cope with negative emotions such as stress, sadness, or boredom. This phenomenon, often called "retail therapy," can lead to impulse purchases that temporarily boost mood but ultimately result in buyer's remorse and financial strain. Recognizing when you're impulse buying is the first step to overcoming it.

- **Tip**: Next time you feel the urge to spend out of impulse, pause and ask yourself., "Does this purchase align with my long-term goals?" Try alternative stress-relief techniques like exercising, journaling, or talking to a friend.

The Pleasure Principle: Spending often triggers the release of dopamine, the brain's "feel-good" chemical. This sensation can create a cycle where you continuously seek the pleasure of making purchases, even if the items you buy don't add long-term value to your life.

- **Solution**: Delayed gratification is the antidote to this pattern. By putting off impulse purchases, you can break the cycle of seeking instant pleasure and focus on long-term satisfaction with bigger financial goals.

The Power of Social Influence: Social media and peer pressure can drive unnecessary spending. Platforms like Instagram, TikTok, and Facebook make it easy to compare yourself to others, and this comparison can lead to spending on things you don't truly need to keep up with trends or appearances.

- **Tip**: Practice mindfulness around social media use and remind yourself that what you see online is often a curated version of reality. Focus on your financial journey and goals rather than comparing yourself to others.

The Anchoring Effect: This cognitive bias occurs when we rely too heavily on the first piece of information we encounter (the "anchor") when making decisions.

For example, if you see a luxury item marked down from $1,000 to $500, you may feel like you're getting a great deal, even if $500 is still more than you intended to spend.

- **Solution**: Be aware of the anchoring effect when shopping and ask yourself if the discounted price fits within your budget. Always focus on the item's value, not just the perceived discount.

Sales Mentality: We have all been saturated with the constant barrage of sales. Save 30% on... etc. This is marketing psychology at work, and it is powerful.

The big BUT, though, is that you are not saving money at all. You are still spending money, and often you are spending money on something you may not have even bought if it were not on sale.

Avoid Bright and Shiney Things: When you have evaluated that you need something then avoid the temptation to buy the most expensive solution to the problem.

- **Example**: There have been more fish caught on a handline than there have on a rod and reel. The fish about to take your bait doesn't care that you have the latest $1000 rod and reel combo. It just sees the bait.

Understanding these psychological triggers will help you develop better spending habits and make more intentional financial decisions.

Delayed Gratification: A Key to *Financial Freedom*

Delayed gratification is resisting the temptation of an immediate reward to achieve a greater reward in the future. It's one of the most powerful skills you can develop on your path to financial success.

It allows you to prioritize saving, and investing, rather than spending money impulsively.

The Science Behind Delayed Gratification:

One of the most well-known demonstrations of delayed gratification is the Stanford marshmallow experiment.

In the original study, children were given a choice: eat one marshmallow immediately or wait and receive two. Early interpretations suggested that those who waited went on to have better outcomes later in life.

More recent research has shown the picture is more complex. Factors like environment, upbringing, and stability play a significant role in those outcomes. In other words, it's not as simple as "wait longer and you'll be more successful."

But the underlying principle still holds.

The ability to pause, consider, and choose a larger future reward over an immediate one is directly relevant to how we manage money. Every financial decision—spending now or saving for later—follows the same pattern.

Practical Ways to Build Delayed Gratification:

1. **Set Clear Goals**: One of the most effective ways to practice delayed gratification is to keep your financial goals at the forefront of your mind. Whether saving for a house, paying off debt, or building an emergency fund, having a tangible goal will make it easier to resist spending impulsively.

2. **Create a Waiting Period**: When you feel the urge to make an unplanned purchase, set a waiting period of at least 24 hours before buying it. This gives you time to consider whether the purchase is essential or just an impulse.

3. **Be Wary**: Advertisers on Facebook and other social media, and even the common Store Sale ads, are all aware of the waiting period technique and craft their ads to instill a sense of urgency in you. The timer ticking down to complete your purchase, the store sale end date, the Black Friday sale, even limiting the number of items available. They are all coercive techniques to overcome your reluctance to buy.

4. **Visualize Your Future Success**: Visualization is a powerful tool in building the habit of delayed gratification. Imagine yourself achieving your financial goals and the satisfaction you'll feel knowing you stayed disciplined. This can help reinforce your commitment to saving rather than spending.

The Rewards of Delayed Gratification: The benefits of practicing delayed gratification go beyond financial gains.

It also fosters a sense of self-discipline, confidence, and control over your life. Each time you successfully resist the temptation to spend, you strengthen your ability to make smarter decisions in the future.

By developing the habit of delayed gratification, you can focus on long-term financial success and avoid the trap of immediate, fleeting satisfaction.

Developing a Positive Money Mindset

Your attitude about money plays a significant role in your financial success. A positive money mindset views money as a tool for achieving your goals rather than a source of stress or fear.

Cultivating the right attitude can transform how you handle your finances and empower you to make smarter decisions.

Shift your mindset from Scarcity to Abundance: Many people operate from a scarcity mindset, which is the belief that there's never enough money.

This mindset leads to fear-based financial decisions, which can create unnecessary stress and hinder one's ability to take risks, save, or invest.

Abundance Mindset: On the other hand, an abundance mindset is the belief that there are endless opportunities to earn and grow wealth. By focusing on abundance, you see money as a tool that works for you rather than something that controls you.

- **Tip**: Start by practicing gratitude for what you have. Rather than focusing on financial struggles, acknowledge the resources and opportunities available to you.
- This shift in perspective can help you develop a healthier relationship with money.

Re-frame Your Financial Challenges as Opportunities: Instead of viewing financial setbacks as failures, start seeing them as learning opportunities.

For example, if you find yourself struggling with debt, ask yourself what led to this situation and how you can use the experience to avoid similar challenges in the future.

- **Tip**: Keep a money journal where you reflect on your financial habits, emotions, and progress. Writing down your thoughts helps identify areas where your mindset may need improvement.

Visualize Financial Success: Visualization is a powerful tool for cultivating a positive money mindset.

Spend a few minutes each day visualizing yourself achieving your financial goals, becoming debt-free, building wealth, or living a financially secure life. Visualization helps you stay motivated and focused on the bigger picture.

Affirmations for Financial Success: Positive affirmations are short, powerful statements that can help rewire your thinking about money.

By repeating affirmations daily, you can shift your mindset and break free from limiting beliefs that hold you back.

Examples of Affirmations:

1. "I am in control of my financial future."
2. "I have the power to earn and grow my wealth."
3. "Money flows to me easily and effortlessly."

- **Tip**: Create your own personalized money affirmations and repeat them each morning.
- This daily practice can boost your confidence and help you develop a more positive outlook on your financial journey.

Surround Yourself with Like-Minded People: The people you spend time with can influence your money mindset. Suppose you surround yourself with individuals focused on building wealth, saving, and achieving financial independence. Their mindset will rub off on you.

Seek out financial communities, online groups, or friends who share your goals.

Learning from Financial Mistakes

No financial journey is perfect, and you will make mistakes (we all have). However, mistakes are a natural part of learning.

Recognizing errors and growing from them is crucial for long-term success.

Using structured worksheets can help break down financial errors, identify contributing factors, and create a plan for improvement.

Key questions to consider:

1. What led to the mistake?
2. What could have been done differently?
3. What steps can prevent a recurrence?

- **Examples**: You signed up for a sure-fire marketing idea that came up via some influencer on social media. It led to a whole raft of unforeseen costs, and huge amounts of time that needed to be spent on it.
- After struggling with it for several months you realised that there was no way you were ever going to have the time or earn the money to make this a success.
- Researching user reviews online to verify if the influencer's positive claims are true and people are getting the touted results.
- It becomes apparent that there are a lot of negative reviews and people were not happy with the results.
- In future more research and a 'sceptical until proven otherwise' mindset will prevent a repeat of this costly mistake.

Staying Motivated During Financial Challenges

Staying motivated on your financial journey can be challenging, especially during difficult times such as economic downturns, unexpected expenses, or personal setbacks. However, maintaining motivation is crucial to reaching your financial goals.

Here are some strategies to help you stay focused and positive, even when the going gets tough.

Break Goals into Smaller Milestones: Large financial goals can feel overwhelming, especially if you're working toward long-term objectives like paying off debt or saving for retirement. To stay motivated, break your goals into smaller, more manageable milestones. For example, if you're trying to save $10,000, focus on saving $1,000 at a time.

Each small success will give you a sense of accomplishment and keep you moving forward.

Celebrate Wins: Celebrating small victories is essential for maintaining motivation. Whether you're paying off a credit card, saving for an emergency fund, or sticking to your budget for three months, take time to acknowledge your progress.

Rewards don't have to be expensive, celebrate by having a relaxing night in or sharing your achievement with a loved one...

Accountability Partners: Find someone you trust as your financial accountability partner. This could be a spouse, friend, family member, or even an online group.

Share your financial goals with them and schedule regular check-ins to discuss your progress. Having someone to hold you accountable can help keep you motivated and focused, especially during tough times.

- **Example**: Lisa and her sister set goals to save $5,000 a year. They checked in with each other monthly, shared their progress, and offered encouragement.
- This accountability system helped them stay on track and meet their savings goals.

Remind Yourself of Your "Why": During difficult times, it's easy to lose sight of why you started your financial journey in the first place.

Take a moment to reflect on your "why." That is the reason behind your financial goals.

Whether providing a better future for your family, achieving financial independence, or living a stress-free life, keeping your "why" in mind will help you push through the challenges.

In a Year, all will be Different: Sometimes, we can get bogged down in the here and now and start to feel defeated.

When this happens just take a moment and remind yourself that this is only temporary. A year from now the issue bugging you will be long past.

By developing a positive money mindset, you'll feel empowered to take control of your financial life, make smarter decisions, and build long-term wealth.

Chapter Four

Building Your Budget

A budget is not a restriction, it's a blueprint for how you want to live your best life

A budget is where things start to come back under control.

Not in theory, in practice. It's where you see what's actually coming in, what's going out, and where it's going wrong.

You can't fix money if you don't know what it's doing.

Whether the goal is to get out of debt, build some breathing room, or stop that constant cycle of one payment chasing another, this is where it begins.

In this chapter, we'll break down how to build a budget that actually works, look at a few different ways to approach it, and go through how to handle both fixed and variable expenses without overcomplicating it.

Budgeting Basics

At its core, a budget is a plan for allocating monthly income. It helps you prioritize essential expenses, identify areas for savings, and control discretionary spending. Let's break down the basic steps of building a budget.

In Chapter 1, you collected all the basics you need to start building your budget. You identified all your income and determined your various fixed and variable expenses, so you are now in an excellent position to develop your budget,

Subtract Expenses from Income: Once you've listed your income and expenses, subtract your total monthly expenses from your total income.

If you have leftover money, that's your disposable income, which can be directed toward saving, investing, or paying off debt. You'll need to adjust your spending if your expenses exceed your income.

Set Savings and Debt Repayment Goals: A budget isn't just about covering your expenses, it's also about achieving your financial goals.

After calculating your basic expenses, decide how much you want to save each month for short-term and long-term goals (such as an emergency fund, a vacation, or retirement).

Similarly, allocate money toward debt repayment if you have any.

Track and Adjust: Budgeting is an ongoing process; tracking your spending is essential.

Monitor your budget each week to ensure you're staying on track and adjust as necessary.

For example, if you overspend in one category, try cutting back in another to balance the budget.

- **Tip**: Some people prefer to track their budget weekly, while others review it at the end of the month.
- Choose the schedule that works best for you, but consistency is key.

By following these steps, you'll have a clear picture of your financial situation and a plan for managing your money effectively.

Popular Budgeting Methods

There are various approaches to budgeting, and different methods work better for different people.

Here are three popular budgeting methods, each with its own benefits.

Zero-Based Budgeting:

This method requires you to assign every dollar of your income to a specific expense or goal so that your income minus expenses equals zero at the end of the month.

In other words, every dollar has a job, whether paying bills, saving, or investing.

How It Works: At the beginning of the month, you list all your expected income and expenses. Once you've allocated money for your fixed and variable expenses, you decide where the remaining money will go, into savings, investments, or debt repayment.

If unexpected expenses arise, you adjust your budget by cutting back in another category.

- **Example**: Sarah uses the zero-based budgeting method. After accounting for her rent, utilities, and groceries, she assigns $300 to savings and $200 to her student loan payments.
- By the end of the month, every dollar has been allocated, and she has zero leftover, meaning she's given every dollar a purpose.

Pros: This method gives you total control over your money and helps ensure you're being intentional with every dollar. It's especially useful for people looking to repay debt or build savings.

Cons: It can be time-consuming to track every expense and make adjustments throughout the month.

50/30/20 Rule:

This simple method divides your after-tax income into three categories:

50% for needs: Essentials like housing, utilities, groceries, insurance, and transportation.

30% for wants: Discretionary spending, such as dining out, entertainment, and travel.

20% for savings and debt repayment: Money set aside for an emergency fund, retirement, or paying off debt.

How It Works: After calculating your monthly take-home income, allocate 50% to your needs, 30% to your wants, and 20% to savings and debt.

This method allows for flexibility while ensuring you're prioritizing your financial goals.

- **Example**: Ben earns $4,000 per month after taxes.
- He allocates $2,000 to his needs, $1,200 to his wants, and $800 to his savings and debt repayment.
- This structure gives him room for fun while ensuring he's building toward his financial goals.

Pros: The 50/30/20 rule is easy to implement and provides flexibility for discretionary spending.

Cons: It may not work well for people with high debt or low income, as the percentages may need adjusting.

Envelope System:

This cash-based system, made popular by financial expert Dave Ramsey, involves physically dividing your money into envelopes labelled with different spending categories.

Once the cash in an envelope is gone, you can't spend any more in that category for the month.

How It Works: At the start of each month, you withdraw cash and allocate it to envelopes marked for specific expenses, such as groceries, dining out, entertainment, and transportation. When an envelope is empty, you stop spending in that category.

- **Example**: Lisa allocates $500 to her "Groceries" envelope, $100 to "Dining Out," and $50 to "Entertainment."
- If she runs out of cash in her Dining Out envelope by mid-month, she can only dine out again in the following month.

Pros: The envelope system is excellent for curbing impulse spending and ensuring you don't overspend in any category.

Cons: Handling cash can be inconvenient and doesn't work well for online shopping or direct deposit payments.

Choose the budgeting method that best fits your lifestyle and financial situation.

The key is consistency, stick to the method that helps you meet your goals while allowing you to enjoy life.

Tools and Apps for Budgeting

With modern technology, managing your budget has never been easier.

Various tools and apps are designed to simplify the budgeting process, making it easy to track your spending, set financial goals, and stay on top of your finances. Here are some of the most popular and effective tools for budgeting.

(As I have previously mentioned, the one caveat I have with these apps is that you are sharing your financial information with a third party, and with that there are inherent risks.)

Mint: Mint is a free budgeting app that connects to your bank accounts and credit cards, automatically tracking your spending and categorizing it for you. Mint provides real-time updates on your spending habits and alerts you when you're close to overspending. It offers insights into where you can save.

1. **Best For**: People who want an easy-to-use, comprehensive app that handles all aspects of budgeting, from tracking expenses to setting goals.
2. **Features**: Expense tracking, goal setting, bill reminders, and credit score monitoring.
3. **Pros**: Free-to-use, real-time tracking, and customizable alerts.
4. **Cons**: Some users report issues with syncing accounts, and ads for financial products can be intrusive.

You Need a Budget (YNAB): YNAB is a paid app ($84/year as at writing) that follows a unique budgeting philosophy: "Give every dollar a job."

YNAB emphasizes proactive budgeting, helping users allocate their money intentionally and focus on long-term financial goals.

1. **Best For**: People looking to get out of debt or take a more hands-on approach to budgeting.
2. **Features**: Detailed expense tracking, goal setting, and personalized budgeting plans.
3. **Pros**: Encourages a proactive approach to budgeting, which is excellent for debt reduction.
4. **Cons**: Requires a subscription fee and has a learning curve for new users.

PocketGuard: PocketGuard simplifies budgeting by showing you how much money you have left to spend after accounting for bills, savings, and goals.

The app connects to your bank accounts and categorizes your spending, helping you see where your money is going and how much you can safely spend.

1. **Best For**: People who want a straightforward app to prevent overspending.
2. **Features**: Expense tracking, bill reminders, and savings goals.
3. **Pros**: Simple and user-friendly, good for avoiding overspending.
4. **Cons**: Fewer features than other budgeting apps, limited customization.

Goodbudget: Goodbudget is a digital version of the envelope system, allowing you to allocate money into virtual envelopes for different spending categories.

It's great for people who like the envelope method but prefer to avoid handling cash.

1. **Best For**: People who like the envelope system and want a digital alternative.
2. **Features**: Virtual envelopes, expense tracking, budget analysis.
3. **Pros**: It helps curb overspending in specific categories and is simple.
4. **Cons**: Lacks real-time syncing with bank accounts.

Spreadsheets: For those who prefer a more manual approach, spreadsheets are a great option.

You can create a custom budgeting spreadsheet in Libre Office, Google Sheets or Excel, allowing you to track income, expenses, and savings in a format tailored to your needs.

1. **Best For**: People who like complete control over their budgeting system and don't mind inputting data manually.

2. **Features**: Fully customizable, allows for complex financial planning.

3. **Pros**: No cost (if using free software like Google Sheets or libre), fully customizable to your specific needs.

4. **Cons**: Requires more manual effort and financial knowledge.

You may already have Excel; if not, you can download the Libre Office Suite for free or use Google Sheets for free.

In Appendix 1 and 2, I have provided the basic step-by-step instructions for setting up your Excel or Libre budgeting spreadsheet.

Whichever tool you choose, the most important thing is consistency.

Regularly tracking your expenses, adjusting your budget, and sticking to your financial plan will ensure long-term success.

Prioritizing Needs vs. Wants

Understanding the difference between needs and wants is fundamental to staying within your budget and making responsible financial decisions. Here's how to differentiate and prioritize:

Needs: Needs are essential expenses that are required for survival and basic well-being. These include:

1. Housing (rent or mortgage payments)

2. Utilities (electricity, water, gas)

3. Groceries and essential food items

4. Health insurance and medical expenses

5. Transportation for work (public transport, car payments)

Wants: Wants are non-essential items that enhance your lifestyle but aren't necessary for basic living. These include:

1. Dining out at restaurants

2. Entertainment (movies, concerts, vacations)

3. Shopping for clothing, gadgets, or luxury items

4. Hobbies and recreational activities

Evaluating Your Expenses: When you're trying to cut costs, start by reviewing your variable expenses and identifying which ones are wants versus needs.

For example, dining out may be a regular expense, but it's something you can reduce by cooking more meals at home.

- **Tip**: When in doubt, ask yourself, "Can I live without this?" If the answer is yes, it's likely a want rather than a need.

Making Trade-Offs: Prioritizing needs over wants doesn't mean you have to cut out all the things you enjoy. Instead, it's about making intentional trade-offs.

For example, you might choose to reduce your dining-out budget so that you can save more for a vacation or build an emergency fund. The key is finding a balance that works for you and aligns with your financial goals.

By understanding the difference between needs and wants, you'll be better equipped to manage your money wisely, avoid overspending, and keep your budget on track.

Chapter Five

Smart Financial Habits

Success is built on the habits you form. Small, consistent actions today will lead to big financial victories tomorrow.

This is where it either sticks, or it doesn't.

A budget helps you get control, but habits are what keep it there. Without them, things drift back to where they were.

It's the small, repeated decisions that make the difference. Saving regularly. Not letting spending creep up as income improves. Keeping an eye on things instead of assuming they're fine.

In this chapter, we'll look at the habits that actually hold everything together, building an emergency fund, saving consistently, avoiding lifestyle creep, managing credit properly, and checking in on your finances often enough to stay on track.

Get these right, and you're not relying on willpower anymore. You've built something that supports itself.

The Importance of an Emergency Fund

An emergency fund is one of the most crucial elements of financial security.

Life is unpredictable, and unexpected expenses, such as medical emergencies, car repairs, or job loss, can arise anytime. Without an emergency fund, you may be forced to rely on credit cards or loans to cover these costs, putting you in debt.

Here's how to build and maintain an emergency fund.

How Much Should You Save? Financial experts typically recommend saving enough to cover three to six months of living expenses. This amount ensures you have a safety net in case of unexpected events, such as losing your job or facing a medical emergency.

- **Tip**: If saving this amount seems overwhelming, start small.
- Even $500 to $1,000 can be a financial buffer against minor emergencies.

Where to Keep Your Emergency Fund: Your emergency fund should be easily accessible but not so easy that you're tempted to dip into it for non-emergencies. An online savings account that can only be accessed online and does not have any credit cards attached to it is a great option.

If you can offset it against your mortgage, even better.

Building the Fund: If you're starting out, focus on building your emergency fund one step at a time. Start by setting aside a small percentage of your income each month.

Automating this process with a direct deposit or recurring transfer to this savings account makes it easier to stay consistent.

By prioritizing your emergency fund, you'll protect yourself from financial setbacks and avoid going into debt when unexpected expenses arise.

Strategies for Consistent Saving

Saving money consistently is one of the most important habits you can develop for financial success.

Even small amounts saved regularly can grow into significant sums over time. Let's explore strategies for building a habit of consistent saving.

Pay Yourself First: One of the most effective saving strategies is to "pay yourself first." This means treating your savings like a non-negotiable expense, like rent or utilities. When you receive your pay, set aside a portion for savings before you spend any money on discretionary items.

Automating this process makes it easier to stick to.

- **Tip**: Set up three accounts.
- One for your emergency fund as described above, one for your savings and one for expenses.
- Along with your emergency funds transfer set up another automatic payment to your savings.
- These should be set up to happen on the same day or day after you receive your pay.
- This will ensure that you save money before you have a chance to spend it elsewhere.

Set Clear Savings Goals: Clear, specific savings goals help you stay motivated and disciplined. Whether saving for an emergency fund, a vacation, a home down payment, or retirement, knowing precisely what you're saving for makes the process easier. Break larger goals into smaller, more manageable steps.

- **Example**: Instead of focusing solely on a long-term goal like saving $50,000 for a home down payment, break it down into short-term goals, such as saving $500 a month.
- You'll feel a sense of accomplishment each time you hit a milestone.

Use the 50/30/20 Rule: If you have a lot of debt and you want to pay that down as a priority, then you might have to adjust these numbers a bit. Following this structure ensures that saving becomes a built-in part of your budget.

Increase Your Savings Rate Over Time: As your income grows, so should your savings rate. If you receive a raise or bonus, avoid the temptation to increase your spending.

Instead, allocate a portion of the increase toward savings.

Save Windfalls: Whenever you receive unexpected money, such as a tax refund, bonus, or gift, consider saving a portion of it. Windfalls are an excellent opportunity to boost your savings quickly without impacting your regular budget.

- **Tip**: Commit to saving at least 50% of any windfall.
- Use the remaining amount to treat yourself or pay off debt.

By developing a habit of consistent saving, you'll steadily build financial security and ensure that you're prepared for both short-term goals and long-term needs.

How to Avoid Lifestyle Inflation

Lifestyle inflation, or lifestyle creep, happens when your spending increases as your income rises.

It's natural to want to upgrade your lifestyle when you start earning more. Still, unchecked lifestyle inflation can prevent you from reaching your financial goals.

Here are strategies to avoid falling into this trap.

Live Below Your Means: One of the simplest ways to avoid lifestyle inflation is to continue living below your means, even as your income increases.

If you receive a raise, avoid the temptation to upgrade your home, car, or lifestyle immediately. Instead, focus on saving more or investing for the future.

- **Example**: After receiving a promotion, David resisted buying a new car and continued driving his reliable, paid-off vehicle.
- By living below his means, he could save for a down payment on a house.

Increase Savings with Income: When your income increases, make it a priority to increase your savings rate as well. Instead of spending the entire raise or bonus, allocate a portion to savings or investments. For example, if you get a 5% raise, increase your savings by 2-3%.

- **Tip**: Try to save at least half of any increase in income. This way, you can still enjoy some extra spending money while making significant progress toward your financial goals.

Set Limits on Discretionary Spending: It's okay to enjoy the fruits of your labor, but set clear limits on how much you'll spend on discretionary items like dining out, vacations, or shopping. Stick to a budget that balances enjoying life with saving for the future.

- **Tip**: Create a separate category in your budget for "fun" spending and commit to sticking within that limit each month.

Avoiding lifestyle inflation will ensure that your income growth leads to greater financial security rather than more expenses.

Developing Good Credit Habits

Your credit score plays a significant role in your financial life.

It affects your ability to get loans, rent an apartment, and even land a job. Good credit habits are essential for maintaining a solid credit profile and ensuring you can borrow money at favorable rates when needed.

Pay Your Bills on Time: Payment history is one of the most significant factors in determining your credit score.

Make it a habit to pay all your bills, credit cards, loans, utilities, on time every month. Late payments can have a significant negative impact on your credit score.

- **Tip**: Set up automatic payments or reminders to ensure you never miss a due date..

Keep Your Credit Utilization Low: Credit utilization refers to the percentage of your available credit that you're using. Keep your credit utilization below 30% to maintain a healthy credit score. For example, if you have a total credit limit of $10,000, aim to use no more than $3,000 of that limit at any given time.

- **Tip**: If your credit card balance regularly approaches your credit limit, consider paying it off more frequently (e.g., biweekly instead of monthly) to keep your utilization low.

Monitor Your Credit Report: Regularly reviewing your credit report helps you stay on top of your credit history and spot any errors or fraudulent activity.

In the US you're entitled to a free credit report once a year from each of the three major credit bureaus (Experian, TransUnion, and Equifax). In other countries it be possible to obtain it even more frequently.

- **Tip**: Use a free service like Credit Karma to monitor your credit score and receive alerts if there are any changes.

Limit New Credit Inquiries: Applying for multiple new credit cards or loans quickly can negatively impact your credit score.

Only apply for new credit when necessary and avoid taking on more debt than you can comfortably handle.

- **Tip**: Before applying for a new credit card, consider how it will affect your credit score and whether you really need the additional credit.

Pay More Than the Minimum: If you carry a balance on your credit cards, aim to pay more than the minimum monthly payment. This reduces your debt faster and saves you money on interest.

- **Example**: By paying $200 a month instead of the $50 minimum on a credit card, you will significantly reduce your debt and save a lot in interest payments.

By developing these credit habits, you'll maintain a strong credit score, which will open up opportunities for lower interest rates and better financial options in the future.

Monitoring and Reviewing Your Financial Health Regularly

Financial health requires consistent monitoring and review.

Regularly reviewing your finances can identify areas for improvement, adjust your goals, and stay on track toward financial success.

Monthly Budget Review: Review your budget and spending at the end of each month. Compare your actual spending to your budgeted amounts and assess whether you stayed within your limits. If you overspent in specific categories, adjust for the following month.

Quarterly Financial Goals Assessment: Assess your progress toward your financial goals every few months. Are you on track to meet your savings targets? If you need to catch up, consider adjusting your budget or timeline to get back on track.

- **Tip**: Set up quarterly check-ins with yourself (or with a financial advisor) to review your progress and make any necessary changes.

Annual Financial Checkup: Conduct a comprehensive financial checkup at least once a year.

Review your savings, investments, debt, and credit score. This is also an excellent time to adjust your long-term financial goals, such as saving for retirement or paying off a mortgage.

- **Tip**: During your annual checkup, review your insurance policies and investment portfolio to ensure they still align with your goals.

Tracking Net Worth: Your net worth is the difference between what you own (assets) and what you owe (liabilities). Tracking your net worth regularly can provide a clear picture of your overall financial health and help you measure progress over time.

- **Tip**: Use a net worth tracking tool or spreadsheet to update your assets and liabilities every quarter.
- This will help you stay motivated and focused on increasing your wealth.

By regularly monitoring your financial health, you can stay proactive, make informed decisions, and ensure that you're consistently moving toward your financial goals.

Chapter Six

Investing in Your Future

Investing isn't just for the wealthy, it's the key to building long-term financial security.

This is where your money starts doing something for you.

Budgeting and saving get things under control. Investing is what moves things forward.

Left alone, money tends to sit still. Invested properly, it starts to work, slowly at first, then more noticeably over time.

This isn't a deep dive into every investment strategy. That would take a book on its own.

What matters here is understanding the basics, how investing fits into the bigger picture, why retirement planning matters earlier than most people think, and how spreading your income sources reduces risk over time.

Investing in Education and Skill Development

One of the most valuable investments you can make is in yourself.

Skills and knowledge compound over time. The more you build, the more opportunities open up.

That might come through formal education, certifications, workshops, or simply learning on your own. The route matters less than the consistency.

- **Technical Skills**: Developing expertise in high-demand fields such as technology, finance, or healthcare can provide a competitive edge.
- **Soft Skills**: Leadership, communication, and problem-solving skills are equally valuable in fostering career growth and business success.

By strategically investing in your education, you not only increase your marketability but also equip yourself with the tools needed to navigate an evolving professional landscape.

Understanding the Basics of Investing

Investing can feel complicated at first—but the basics are straightforward.

Once you understand how it works, it becomes a lot easier to see where it fits.

Let's break down some core concepts to help you understand how investing works.

What is Investing? Investing is simply putting your money into assets that have the potential to grow over time.

These assets include stocks, bonds, real estate, precious metals, and businesses.

Investing aims to earn a return on your money through appreciation (the value of the asset increases) or income (such as dividends or interest).

The Power of Compound Interest: One of the biggest advantages of investing is compounding interest, which means you earn interest not only on your original investment but also on the interest it has already earned.

This creates a snowball effect, your money grows at an accelerating rate over time.

- **Example**: If you invest $1,000 with an annual return of 7%, you'll have $1,070 after one year.
- In the second year, you'll earn 7% on $1,070, giving you $1,144.90.

- Over time, this compounding effect can significantly grow your wealth.

Risk vs. Reward: Every investment carries some level of risk, there's always a chance of loss.

Generally, higher-risk investments offer the potential for higher returns. In contrast, lower-risk investments tend to provide more stability but lower returns.

Understanding your risk tolerance, how comfortable you are with the possibility of losing money, is critical to choosing suitable investments.

- **Tip**: Spreading your money across different types of investments can help reduce risk and smooth out the ups and downs. .

There are a few main types of investments you'll come across:

Stocks: When you buy a stock, you're purchasing a small share of ownership in a company.

If the company does well, the value of your stock may increase, and you could also receive dividends (a share of the company's profits).

Bonds: Bonds are essentially loans you give to companies or governments.

In return, they agree to pay you interest over a period and return your principal investment. Bonds are generally considered safer than stocks but offer lower returns.

Mutual Funds and ETFs: Mutual and exchange-traded funds (ETFs) allow you to invest in a diversified portfolio of stocks or bonds.

These funds pool money from multiple investors and are managed by professionals. ETFs are traded on stock exchanges like individual stocks. At the same time, mutual funds are bought directly from the company managing the fund.

Precious Metals: Investing in gold and silver has long been regarded as a reliable way to preserve wealth and diversify a portfolio.

These precious metals are often considered safe-haven assets, particularly during times of economic uncertainty or market volatility. Gold and silver can effectively hedge against inflation, as their value typically rises when fiat currency's purchasing power declines.

Additionally, these metals have intrinsic value, are globally recognized, and offer a tangible asset that does not rely on the performance of any specific company or government. For long-term investors, holding gold and silver can provide stability and serve as a buffer against broader market downturns.

A Word of Caution.

Gold and silver have their place, but they're not magic. They don't produce income—no dividends, no interest. What you're relying on is price movement.

That price is driven by sentiment, supply and demand, and broader economic conditions. It can move quickly in either direction.

If you're holding the physical metal, there are also costs, storage, insurance, and those eat into returns.

They can act as a hedge against inflation, but not consistently. Sometimes they track it. Sometimes they lag it. Sometimes they run ahead of it.

Used properly, they can strengthen a portfolio. Just don't treat them as the whole strategy.

Crypto Currency: Cryptocurrency is a newer and more volatile area of investing.

It involves digital assets like Bitcoin or Ethereum, which can move quickly in both directions. The potential upside draws people in—but so does the risk.

There are thousands of tokens, and many won't last. That makes understanding what you're investing in, and how you're storing it, especially important.

If you choose to include crypto, treat it carefully. Keep it as part of a broader strategy, not the whole plan..

It's also worth keeping an eye on regulation, this is an area that changes quickly, and the rules don't always stay still.

Understanding these basic concepts will equip you to make informed decisions and build your investment portfolio.

Affordable Ways to Start Investing

You don't need a large sum of money to start investing.

Thanks to advancements in technology, investing has become more accessible than ever. Let's explore some affordable ways to get started.

Robo-Advisors: Robo-advisors are automated investment platforms that create and manage a diversified portfolio based on your financial goals and risk tolerance. They're an excellent option for beginners who want a hands-off approach to investing.

1. **Example**: Popular robo-advisors like Betterment, Wealthfront, and SoFi Invest allow you to start investing with as little as $100. These platforms use algorithms to build a portfolio of stocks, bonds, and other assets tailored to your financial situation.

2. **Pros**: Low fees, automated management, and diversification. Ideal for beginners.

3. **Cons**: Less flexibility if you prefer to pick individual stocks or investments.

Fractional Shares: In the past, you had to buy whole shares of stocks, which could be expensive.

Today, many brokerage platforms allow you to purchase fractional shares, meaning you can invest in big companies like Amazon or Tesla for as little as $5.

1. **Example**: Robinhood, Fidelity, and Charles Schwab offer fractional share investing, allowing you to start small and build your portfolio over time.

2. **Pros**: Low entry cost, allows you to invest in high-value companies.

3. **Cons**: It still requires research and understanding of individual stocks.

Exchange-Traded Funds (ETFs): ETFs are an excellent option for new investors because they offer diversification at a low cost.

Instead of picking individual stocks, you can invest in an ETF that tracks a broad index like the S&P 500, exposing you to hundreds of companies with a single investment.

1. **Example**: Vanguard's S&P 500 ETF (VOO) is a popular choice for beginners looking for exposure to the U.S. stock market.
2. **Pros**: Low fees, diversification, and easier to manage than individual stocks.
3. **Cons**: Returns depend on the overall market performance, so risk is still involved.

Employer-Sponsored Retirement Plans: If your employer offers a retirement plan like a 401(k), this is one of the most accessible and affordable ways to start investing.

Many employers provide matching contributions, meaning they'll match a portion of your contributions.

- **Tip**: Even if you need to figure out how much you can afford to contribute, aim to contribute at least enough to get the match. You can always increase your contributions as your income grows.

By taking advantage of these affordable investment options, you can start building your wealth even if you have little money to invest upfront.

Retirement Planning for Cost-Saving

Retirement planning is one of the most critical aspects of financial planning.

The earlier you start saving for retirement, the more time your money has to grow through compound interest, making it easier to reach your retirement goals.

Start Early: The earlier you begin saving for retirement, the better. Time is your biggest asset in retirement planning because of the power of compound interest. Even small contributions made in your 20s can grow into a significant nest egg when you retire.

- **Example**: If you start saving $200 a month at age 25 and earn an average annual return of 7%, you'll have over $500,000 by age 65.
- If you wait until age 35 to start, you'll only have around $240,000 by retirement, assuming the same savings rate and return.

Choose Low-Cost Investment Options: Many retirement accounts offer various investment options. Look for low-cost index funds or ETFs, which typically have lower fees and can provide broad market exposure.

Minimizing fees can have a substantial impact on overall returns over time.

- **Tip**: Avoid expensive, actively managed funds unless you're confident they can outperform their benchmarks after accounting for fees.

Set Retirement Goals: Determine how much you'll need to retire comfortably by estimating your future expenses and the lifestyle you want to maintain.

Use retirement calculators to calculate how much you need to save each month to reach your goal.

- **Tip**: Revisit your retirement goals periodically and adjust your savings plan based on changes in your financial situation or retirement plans.

By starting early, maximizing employer contributions, and investing in low-cost options, you can build a solid foundation for a financially secure retirement.

Diversifying Income Streams

In addition to investing in the stock market, diversifying your income streams is another powerful way to build long-term financial security.

Relying on a single source of income, such as your primary job, can be risky, especially if economic circumstances change. Diversification can provide you with multiple streams of income that help safeguard your financial future.

Side Hustles: A side hustle can be anything from freelancing to starting an online business. Platforms like Upwork, Fiverr, and Etsy make monetizing your skills and passions easier.

Even if your side hustle generates a small amount of income, it can help you reach your financial goals faster.

- **Tip**: Choose a side hustle that aligns with your skills and interests so that it feels enjoyable rather than burdensome.
- **Tip**: Be very careful when looking at online offers of side hustles.
- There is a plethora of them bombarding Facebook pages and social media these days.
- Many are cleverly disguised Mass Marketing Schemes, and most hide the amount of work and the actual cost to you of software, support, advertising, stockholding, or just the amount of time you need to spend for little to no return.
- Some are just pure scams where you sign up. Then they have your Credit card details and enough personal information to steal your identity.

Rental Income: If you have extra space in your home or a property you're not using, consider renting it out.

Platforms like Airbnb allow you to rent out rooms or entire properties to travelers, providing an additional income stream. Or you could take in a boarder to help pay down your mortgage and share utility costs.

- **Tip**: Air BnB may be problematic in your city, and you need to understand any city ordinances around this short-term accommodation option.
- **Tip**: When determining the amount you will charge for the board, you need to apportion all your utility costs, any food included, your mortgage payment, city taxes, etc. Then, they should be apportioned relatively over the number of occupants.

Dividend Income: If you invest in dividend-paying stocks, you can generate a passive income stream.

Dividends are payments made by companies to shareholders, typically quarterly. By building a portfolio of dividend-paying stocks, you can create a steady source of passive income over time.

- **Tip**: Reinvest your dividends to buy more shares and benefit from compounding.
- Over time, this can significantly increase your portfolio's value.

Real Estate Investments: Real estate is another way to diversify your income streams.

You don't have to buy an entire property to get started, real estate investment trusts (REITs) allow you to invest in real estate without owning physical property. REITs pool investors' money to buy, manage, and sell income-generating properties like commercial buildings, apartments, and warehouses.

- **Tip**: Look for REITs with a history of stable dividends and low management fees.

Diversifying your income streams will create additional revenue sources to provide financial stability and accelerate wealth-building efforts.

Chapter Seven

Cost-Saving Strategies in Everyday Life

Small changes can make significant gains

Most people think saving money means cutting things out.
It usually doesn't.

More often, it's about paying attention, spotting where money slips away and tightening things without turning life into a grind.

Small changes add up. Not once, but over and over again. That's where the difference is made.

In this chapter, we'll look at practical ways to do that, simple adjustments, everyday decisions, and a few areas most people overlook that can make an immediate difference.

Thrift Shopping and Second-Hand Buying

Buying second-hand is one of the easiest ways to save money on everything from clothes to furniture.

Thrift shopping allows you to find high-quality, gently used items at a fraction of their original cost. Let's explore how to make the most of thrift stores and second-hand shopping.

Clothing: Thrift stores and online platforms like Poshmark, Depop, and ThredUp offer second-hand clothing in excellent condition, often at a fraction of retail prices. You can find designer brands, vintage pieces, and everyday wear at significantly reduced prices.

- **Tip**: When thrift shopping for clothing, inspect items carefully for any damage (stains, missing buttons, etc.) and try everything on if possible.
- Look for sales days or clearance events at your local thrift store for even deeper discounts.
- **For example,** One woman I know built a stylish wardrobe by shopping at second-hand stores. She saved hundreds of dollars by purchasing designer clothes that would have cost her significantly more at department stores.
- Another was the opposite; she had a severe impulse-buying problem and would periodically take bags of clothes she had often never worn (still had the labels on them) to donate to thrift stores.

Furniture: Buying used furniture can save you hundreds or even thousands of dollars. Platforms like Facebook Marketplace, Craigslist, and local thrift stores often have high-quality furniture at a fraction of the cost of buying new.

Before purchasing, check for signs of wear and tear or damage.

- **Tip**: If you're crafty, you can often refinish or repaint used furniture to give it new life.
- A fresh coat of paint or new hardware can transform a thrift store find into a piece that fits perfectly in your home.

Electronics and Appliances: Many second-hand stores or websites sell refurbished electronics, such as laptops, phones, and kitchen appliances.

Refurbished items are often much cheaper than new ones, and many come with warranties for added peace of mind.

- **Example**: Tom purchased a refurbished laptop from an online retailer, saving $300 compared to buying it new. It came with a one-year warranty.

Household Items: Thrift stores and second-hand shops are also great places to find household goods like dishes, cookware, and home decor.

Many items are gently used or even new, allowing you to furnish your home for a fraction of what you'd spend at traditional retailers.

- **Tip**: If you're moving into a new apartment or home, check second-hand stores first for essentials like plates, utensils, and furniture.
- You'll be surprised by the quality and selection available at a much lower cost.

Thrift shopping and buying second-hand saves money and supports sustainability by giving items a second life. With patience and creativity, you can find amazing deals on high-quality items while keeping more money in your pocket.

DIY *Options for Home and Personal Care*

One of the best ways to cut costs is to take a DIY approach to home maintenance and personal care. This not only saves money but also gives you more control over the products and services you use.

Home Repairs and Maintenance: Many minor home repairs and maintenance tasks can be done without hiring a professional.

Most homeowners can handle straightforward jobs like painting, fixing leaky faucets, and patching small holes in walls with some research.

- **Tip**: YouTube is a valuable resource for learning how to do minor repairs yourself.
- Tutorials from professionals can guide you through the process step by step, saving you the cost of hiring a contractor.
- **Example**: Instead of paying a plumber a lot of money to fix a leaky faucet, you could watch a tutorial online and do it yourself for the cost of the replacement parts, just a few dollars.

DIY Cleaning Products: Making your own cleaning supplies is cost-effective and environmentally friendly. Many homemade cleaning solutions use common household ingredients like vinegar, baking soda, and essential oils.

These are cheaper and can be safer than store-bought cleaners filled with harsh chemicals.

- **Tip**: Combine equal parts vinegar and water for an all-purpose cleaner that works on most surfaces.
- For tougher stains, use baking soda as a scrubbing agent.

Personal Care: DIY personal care products, such as face masks, body scrubs, and hair treatments, can save you money and allow you to control their ingredients.

- **Example**: You can create a sugar scrub using sugar, coconut oil, and essential oils.
- It will cost just a few dollars to make and works just as well as expensive store-bought scrubs.

Gardening: If you have the space, growing your vegetables and herbs can save you money on groceries.

Even small container gardens on a balcony or windowsill can yield fresh produce, reducing the need to buy expensive herbs or specialty vegetables.

- **Tip**: Start with easy-to-grow herbs like basil, mint, or parsley.
- These plants require little maintenance and can be grown indoors or outdoors.

By taking on more DIY projects, you'll save money and feel accomplished when completing tasks yourself.

Couponing, Discount Hunting, and Cashback Programs

Coupons and discounts are simple ways to save money on everyday purchases. With the rise of digital couponing and cashback programs, it's easier than ever to find deals that reduce the cost of groceries, household items, and even large purchases.

Couponing: Traditional paper and digital coupons are widely available through newspapers, store websites, and couponing apps. Many stores offer digital coupons that can be applied by scanning your phone at checkout.

Discount Codes and Sales: When shopping online, always check for discount codes before purchasing.

Websites like RetailMeNot and Honey provide discount codes for thousands of retailers. Retailers also offer sales during holidays, back-to-school season, or clearance events where you can find great discounts on various items.

- **Tip**: Before making any online purchase, quickly search for discount codes to see if you can reduce the price.
- Browser extensions like Honey will automatically search for and apply any available discounts at checkout.

Cashback Apps: Cashback programs allow you to earn money back on your purchases. Apps like Rakuten, Ibotta, and Fetch Rewards offer cash back when you shop through their links or upload receipts. These programs often partner with grocery stores, clothing retailers, and online platforms, allowing you to earn cash back on almost any purchase.

Price Matching and Price Comparison: Many stores offer price matching, which means they'll match a lower price you find at a competitor. Before making large purchases, compare prices online to find the best deal.

- **Tip**: Use price comparison websites like Google Shopping or PriceGrabber to quickly find the lowest price available.
- Once you find a lower price, ask your preferred store if they'll match it.
- The main street store will have had to have carried the stock in-store, and they have the added cost of the store etc, so it may not be in their interest to match an online price.
- But on the other hand, depending on whether you have free shipping, or not, from the online store this may swing the deal to the shopfront.

Loyalty Programs: Some stores offer loyalty programs that reward frequent shoppers with discounts, points, or cashback offers.

By signing up for these programs, you can earn rewards on purchases you're already making and redeem them for future savings.

Air travel: Possibly, the majority of people use online booking services these days to book their air travel and accommodation.

If, like me, you are one of those, use several different sites and compare their offerings so you can get the most cost-effective deal.

- **Tip:** Something to consider is when booking a round trip whether a number of one-way legs may end up cheaper.
- **Example**: I wanted to travel from Perth to Bali, and then on to Singapore and back to Perth.
- Doing my research, I got a quote for the round trip and then started to break it down into single legs.
- I then found that by doing it this way, there was a flight direct from Bali to Singapore that had not come up on the round trip.
- Taking that option, saved about $300 per person, and as there were two of us traveling, that was $600 dollars in my pocket.

By making couponing, discount hunting, and cashback programs part of your routine, you'll consistently save money on purchases of all sizes.

The Power of Negotiation: How to Ask for Lower Rates

Negotiating lower rates on bills, services, and even big-ticket purchases can save you hundreds, if not thousands, of dollars each year.

Many people shy away from negotiating, but the truth is that many companies are willing to offer discounts, if you ask.

Negotiating Utility Bills: It may surprise you, but utility companies (especially cable, internet, and phone providers) are often willing to negotiate lower rates to retain loyal customers. If your bill has increased, or you find a better deal with a competitor, call your current provider and ask if they can offer a lower rate.

- **Tip**: Be polite but firm. Mention that you've been a loyal customer and ask if they can match or beat a competitor's rate.

Medical Bills: Many healthcare providers and hospitals are willing to negotiate payment plans or reduce charges if you're struggling to pay a medical bill. If you receive a large medical bill, contact the billing department to ask if they can reduce the amount or set up an affordable payment plan.

- **Tip**: Check your medical bills for errors, such as duplicate charges or services you didn't receive.
- If you find any discrepancies, contact the billing office to dispute them.

Big Purchases: When buying expensive items like furniture, appliances, or electronics, don't be afraid to negotiate.

Many retailers are willing to offer discounts or throw in additional perks (like free delivery) if you ask.

- **Tip**: Research prices online before negotiating to ensure you're getting a fair deal.
- Mentioning competitor prices can give you leverage during negotiations.

Tax Liabilities: If you have managed to fall behind with your filings or, through a windfall or random circumstance, ended up with a large tax bill, contact the Tax office and arrange a payment plan. This way, you will avoid penalties if you stick to the plan.

By learning the art of negotiation, you can reduce costs from monthly bills to major purchases, putting more money back in your pocket.

Chapter Eight

Life and Disability Insurance: Protecting What Matters Most

Live for the best but prepare for the worst.

This is the cost most people don't want to think about, let alone pay for.

Insurance feels like dead money. You pay it, hope you never use it, and quietly question whether it's worth it.

The problem is, when something does go wrong, it's rarely small. It's the kind of event that can undo everything you've built if you're not protected.

Budgeting and saving help you stay in control day to day. Insurance is what protects you when things fall apart.

In this chapter, we'll look at where life and disability insurance fit, what they actually do, and why ignoring them can end up costing far more than the premiums ever will.

Why Life Insurance?

Life insurance is a contract between you and an insurer that guarantees a payment to your beneficiaries upon your passing in exchange for regular premium payments. Its primary purpose is financially supporting your dependents if you pass away unexpectedly.

Here's why it matters:

Income Replacement: If your family depends on your income, life insurance ensures they can maintain their standard of living, covering daily expenses, housing costs, and future needs like education.

Debt Protection: Life insurance can help pay off significant debts, such as a mortgage or personal loans, sparing your family from financial stress during an already difficult time.

Final Expenses: Funeral and burial costs can be surprisingly high, often exceeding $10,000. Life insurance can cover these costs, so your family isn't burdened.

Legacy Building: Some policies allow you to leave a financial legacy, supporting your heirs or a cause close to your heart.

Types of Life Insurance

There are two primary types of life insurance, each suited to different needs:

Term Life Insurance: This is the simplest and most affordable option.

It provides coverage for a set term (e.g., 10, 20, or 30 years).

If you outlive the term, the policy expires with no payout. Still, the premiums are typically much lower than permanent insurance.

Permanent Life Insurance: This includes whole life, universal life, and variable life insurance.

These policies last your entire lifetime and often have a cash value that grows over time, which you can borrow against or withdraw. However, premiums are higher.

Choosing the right policy depends on your budget, goals, and the financial needs of your dependents. A term policy may be sufficient for families looking for affordable protection during their working years, while permanent policies can offer additional benefits for those with complex estate planning needs.

The Importance of Disability Insurance

Disability insurance is equally critical but often overlooked.

It replaces a portion of your income if you cannot work due to illness or injury.

Here's why it's essential:

Income Continuation: Your ability to earn an income is one of your most valuable assets.

Disability insurance ensures you can cover your financial obligations, even if you can't work.

Covers Long-Term Needs: While many assume short-term savings or employer benefits will suffice, long-term disabilities often last months or years.

Disability insurance fills this gap.

Protects Your Goals: Without disability insurance, an extended period without income can derail retirement savings, children's education funds, and other financial plans.

Types of Disability Insurance

There are two main types of disability insurance:

Short-Term Disability (STD): Provides income replacement for temporary disabilities, typically lasting three to six months.

Many employers offer STD coverage as part of their benefits package.

Long-Term Disability (LTD): Kicks in after a waiting period (usually 90 days or more) and can last for years or even until retirement. Individual policies are available if your employer does not offer LTD.

When evaluating policies, look for those with an **"own occupation" definition**. This means benefits are paid if you cannot perform your specific job, even if you could do other types of work.

Budgeting for Insurance

Including life and disability insurance in your budget is critical for financial security. While premiums may feel like an added expense, they provide invaluable peace of mind. Here are some tips for fitting insurance into your budget:

Start Early: Premiums are generally lower when you're younger and healthier, so purchase policies as soon as possible.

Bundle Policies: Some insurers offer discounts for bundling life and disability insurance or other policies like home and auto insurance.

Choose the Right Coverage Amount: Avoid over-insuring. Calculate how much your dependents would need to cover essential expenses and tailor your policy accordingly.

Review Policies Regularly: Life changes, such as marriage, having children, or a career shift, may necessitate adjustments to your coverage.

Overcoming Common Objections

Many people delay purchasing life and disability insurance due to misconceptions:

"I'm too young." Accidents and illnesses don't discriminate by age; younger people often get the best rates.

"It's too expensive." While permanent policies can be costly, term life and individual disability insurance policies are often affordable, especially when purchased early.

"I don't need it; I'm healthy." While good health is a blessing, unexpected events can still happen.

Insurance provides a safety net, you hope you never need it, but you'll be glad it's there if you do

Building Peace of Mind

Life and disability insurance are not just about preparing for the worst; they're about ensuring your family and financial goals are protected no matter what life throws your way.

By including these policies in your financial plan, you're investing in security, stability, and peace of mind.

Prioritize protecting what matters most, and you'll lay the foundation for a financially resilient future.

Chapter Nine

Understanding Taxation in Personal Finance

Give unto Caesar that which is Caesars, and not a penny more

This is the part no one enjoys, but it matters.

Taxes quietly shape how much of your money you actually keep. Ignore them, and they'll catch up with you.

You don't need to become an expert, but you do need to understand how they affect your income, your decisions, and your overall position.

This chapter breaks down the basics so you can see what's going on, and avoid a few expensive surprises.

What Are Taxes and Why Do They Matter?

Taxes are money you're required to pay to the government—whether you like it or not. These payments to the government are supposed to fund public services, such as infrastructure, healthcare, and education. Understanding the types of taxes and their implications on your income is vital for financial planning.

Key Types of Taxes

You'll come across a few common types.

Some are obvious (Like the amount deducted as payroll tax from your pay), and others only become obvious once you become liable for them (such as property or capital gains tax). No matter what type they are, you can guarantee that the government will want its share of any income you generate.

Income Tax: Levied on wages, salaries, and investment returns. It may include federal, state, and local taxes.

Sales Tax, GST (Goods and Services Tax), Or VAT if you are in Britain: These taxes are applied to goods and services at the point of purchase.

Property Tax: Based on the value of property you own, such as real estate.

Payroll Tax: Withheld from your paycheck to fund Government programs.

Capital Gains Tax: Imposed on the profit from selling investments .

Apart from these, other Government charges must be paid.

They are cleverly disguised as fees and levies and, in some instances, will mainly go to State and Local governments, but some are also Federal charges.

Common ones are:

Vehicle License or Registration: Charged to register your vehicle and, in some countries, includes a third-party insurance component.

Fishing and Hunting Licences: Yes, if you want to fish or hunt in general, you will have to pay for a license to allow you to do so.

Alcohol and Tobacco Taxes are paid at the production level, and then the cost is passed on to you, the consumer, in the form of vastly inflated purchase prices.

Luxury Vehicle or Goods Tax: There is always someone sitting in a back office somewhere in the government dreaming up ways to get another dollar out of you.

So why not add extra charges to what they deem luxury items? They think that if you can afford the item, you can surely afford to pay the government an additional 10, 20, or more, percent for it.

Stamp Duty: Fees charged for registering a contract or change of title for real estate or other instruments.

How Taxes Affect Your Budget

Taxes directly impact your take-home pay and disposable income.

It's crucial to account for taxes when budgeting to avoid surprises. The following are the key concepts you need to understand.

Gross vs. Net Income: Gross income is your total earnings before taxes, while net income is what remains after deductions.

Marginal Tax Rate: Most countries work on a sliding tax scale.

This means your first set amount may be tax-free, the next amount at, say, 10 percent, then 20 percent, etc., up until you reach the maximum tax bracket.

So, your **marginal** tax rate is the tax percentage applied to your last dollar of income.

Effective Tax Rate: This is the **average** rate you pay on your total income, considering all sources and deductions based on the sliding scale of tax brackets you are levied as above.

- **Example:** Your income may be high enough that some of your income may be taxable at the highest marginal tax rate.
- But once you average all your tax liability, your effective tax rate will be lower than this.
- This is how your employer decides how to withhold your payroll tax. They take your estimated total earnings over the year, apply the various tax brackets to it, and then apply this calculated **effective** tax rate.
- It also explains why you do not necessarily get a linear return in your pay packet

if you are paid for overtime. Because each pay they treat as if this is what you will earn for the rest of the year.

- Some of that overtime pay might have pushed you into a theoretically higher tax bracket.

Tax Planning Strategies

Smart tax planning can help reduce your tax liability and free up resources for other financial goals.

Various things can be used to reduce your tax liability. However, the best way is to engage a tax accountant who you can trust and get their advice.

There have been numerous loopholes created and exploited by bright individuals only to have the various governments shut them down, and the individuals using them end up with substantial tax liabilities.

Tax laws keep changing constantly, and there is little chance that an individual can keep up with these changes and their implications. You have a tax accountant for that, as you are paying for their knowledge to protect you.

If you need clarification, call them and ask about the implications of what you are considering doing.

- **Example**: I had a portfolio of Crypto holdings across various tokens.
- On advice from a so-called investment firm, I sold some of my high-performance tokens and moved the proceeds to "sure thing" Alt Coins.
- I had a huge tax liability because I had made a decent capital gain on the tokens I sold.
- If I had spoken to my accountant, he would have advised me to hold and not change course.
- Or sell my under-performing tokens and use the capital loss from those to offset the capital gain on the sold tokens.

Tax Filing and Compliance

Filing taxes accurately and on time is essential to avoid penalties.

As various countries use different reporting periods, it is vital to know these requirements. Then, you have the choice as to how to prepare and file your tax return.

Do-It-Yourself: Online tax software like TurboTax or H&R Block May be helpful.

Hire a Professional: A tax filing bureau will be adequate for simple returns where you mainly earn income from a salary and perhaps a side hustle generating little income. However, for complex tax situations or higher incomes, you really need an accredited tax accountant.

Managing Taxes Throughout the Year

Tax management isn't just a once-a-year task. Incorporate it into your financial routine:

Track deductible expenses consistently. Gather all your receipts for valid expenditure.

Keep and print out all your bank statements and record any interest payments.

If you are self-employed and the taxation department has levied a withholding tax payment plan, or you have entered into an arrears payment plan with them, ensure you remit the required amount on time. Penalty fines and interest charges can quickly get out of control.

Be aware that some expenses are not claimable as a one-off payment but are claimed via depreciation over several years.

- **Example**: You have a rental property, and you replace the carpets as they were old and worn.
- You will likely be unable to claim this cost as an expense as the taxation office deems it an improvement.
- However, you can claim the approved depreciation rate on this carpet replacement in the following years.

- **Conversely**: Your rental unit has a broken toilet, and you call a plumber to replace the cistern.

- This is an expense and can be claimed as such.

Get a handle on this, and you avoid unnecessary stress, and keep more of your money working where it should.

Chapter Ten

Additional Ways to Cut Costs

Cutting costs does not mean cutting happiness; it's about finding more efficient ways to manage your money

By now, you've probably dealt with the obvious expenses.

This is where the less obvious ones start to show up. The small things, the overlooked ones, the bits that don't feel like much on their own, but add up over time.

Subscriptions that quietly renew. Travel that costs more than it needs to. Spending that creeps in because it's convenient.

In this chapter, we'll look at a few of those areas and how to tighten them up without turning everything into a restriction.

Subscriptions and Memberships: What to Keep and What to Cut

With so many subscription services available today, signing up for things you don't fully use or need is easy.

Over time, these small monthly charges can add up and significantly drain your budget. Here's how to audit your subscriptions and memberships to save money:

Conduct a Subscription Audit: Start by making a list of every subscription you have, whether it's a streaming service, a gym membership, a meal kit, or a monthly delivery service.

Review your bank statements and credit card bills to ensure you capture everything.

- **Tip**: Ask yourself if you're getting enough value from each subscription.

Cancel Unused Subscriptions: Once you've listed your subscriptions, cancel anything you're not using regularly.

Many subscription services have "pause" options, allowing you to stop the service temporarily instead of canceling it outright. This can be a good option if you want to return to it later.

- **Example**: If you last used your gym membership a few months ago, consider canceling it or switching to a cheaper alternative.

Look for Bundle Deals: Many companies offer bundle deals that combine several services at a lower price.

- **Example:** If you subscribe to multiple streaming services, look for packages with multiple platforms for one fee, such as Disney+ bundled with Hulu and ESPN+.
- **Tip**: Telecom companies sometimes bundle phone, internet, and TV services at a lower rate, so it's worth checking if bundling services with one provider can save you money.

Share Subscriptions: Some services allow family or friends to share accounts. Check the terms of service to ensure you're not violating any usage rules.

Regularly reviewing your subscriptions and memberships can cut unnecessary expenses and keep only the services that bring real value to your life.

Traveling on a Budget

Travel doesn't have to be expensive, and with the right planning, you can explore new destinations without breaking the bank.

Here are some practical ways to save on travel:

Travel Off-Peak: Traveling during the off-season or shoulder season (between peak and off-peak seasons) can save you a lot on flights, accommodation, and activities. Not only are prices lower, but tourist spots are less crowded, allowing for a more enjoyable experience.

Use Flight Comparison Tools: Websites like Google Flights, Skyscanner, and Bookin g.com allow you to compare flight prices across multiple airlines. These platforms also let you set price alerts to monitor fare changes and book when prices drop.

- **Tip**: Be flexible with your travel dates.
- Flying mid-week is often cheaper than flying on weekends.
- Adjusting your departure or return date by a few days can result in significant savings.

Stay in Budget Accommodations: Instead of booking a hotel, consider more affordable options like Airbnb, hostels, or even staying with friends and family.

Many hostels offer private rooms at lower rates than hotels, providing both affordability and privacy.

Travel Insurance: When booking travel and accommodation, remember your travel insurance.

Often, the best rates are available on the booking service you use. This is essential as a minor accident at home is one thing, but the same accident in another country can be extremely costly.

Most times, your home-based medical insurance does not cover overseas travel.

Eat Like a Local: Dining out at touristy restaurants can quickly eat into your travel budget. Save money by eating at local spots, street food vendors, or markets. You'll often find delicious, authentic food at a fraction of the price of dining at tourist restaurants.

- **Tip**: If your accommodation has a kitchen, consider buying groceries and cook some of your meals to save even more.

Use Public Transportation: Instead of relying on taxis or rental cars, use public transportation like buses, subways, or trains. Not only is this cheaper, but it also provides a more authentic travel experience.

- **Tip**: In many cities, purchasing a transportation pass for a day or week can offer unlimited rides at a discounted rate compared to paying for individual trips.
- Following these tips, you can enjoy travel experiences without overspending and still have memorable adventures.

The Sharing Economy: Leveraging Services like Carpooling

The sharing economy has made saving money by sharing resources more straightforward than ever.

Leveraging platforms that connect people looking to share rides, homes, and other goods or services can cut costs significantly.

Carpooling and Ridesharing: Using rideshare services like Uber or Lyft is a common way to get around.

However, the shared ride option (UberPool or Lyft Shared) can reduce costs. Look into carpooling services or apps like Waze Carpool that match drivers and riders going in the same direction for regular commutes.

- **Example**: By carpooling to work, you will reduce your monthly transportation costs and save on fuel and parking fees.

Tool and Equipment Sharing: Instead of buying expensive tools or equipment you'll only use once or twice, ask around your friends and family. Often, they will have what you need for the one-off time you need it. Just ensure you do not break the trust by returning it dirty or broken.

- **Example**: My brother-in-law borrowed my blower/vac. When he returned it, he had clogged it with shredded newspaper from cleaning out his guinea pig hutch.

He had also burnt out the motor, and I had to replace the unit. Not good!

Car Sharing: If you don't drive often but still need a car occasionally, some places offer car-sharing services like Zipcar or Turo.

These platforms let you rent cars by the hour or more. You can also often find online companies like Rent a Wreck that have serviceable vehicles that are not exactly up to the standard of the majors but are adequate for short-term hire.

- **Tip**: Use these services only when necessary. Public transportation or biking is more cost-effective for short trips or errands.

By taking advantage of the sharing economy, you can save on everyday expenses and large purchases while benefiting from more sustainable consumption practices.

Minimalism and Downsizing

Minimalism is a lifestyle philosophy that promotes living with less.

By focusing on what you truly need and letting go of excess, you can save money, reduce stress, and live more intentionally. Here's how embracing minimalism and downsizing can help you cut costs:

Declutter and Sell Unused Items: Start by decluttering your home and selling items you no longer need.

Sites like eBay, Facebook Marketplace, and Craigslist make it easy to sell gently used items. Decluttering clears your space and puts extra cash in your pocket.

Buy Less, Choose Quality: Minimalism encourages intentional spending. Instead of buying many cheap, disposable items, focus on purchasing fewer, higher-quality items that will last longer.

While the upfront cost may be higher, you'll save money in the long run by avoiding frequent replacements.

- **Tip**: Apply this principle to clothing, electronics, and home goods.

- Opt for well-made items that offer durability and value over time.

Downsize Your Living Space: I covered this previously, but it is worth repeating.

Embrace Experiences Over Things: Minimalism also emphasizes valuing experiences over material possessions.

Instead of spending money on things you don't need, focus on creating meaningful experiences like traveling, spending time with loved ones, or pursuing hobbies.

- **Tip**: Before purchasing, ask yourself if the item will genuinely add value to your life.
- If not, consider putting that money toward an experience you'll remember and cherish.

DIY: Some things require a professional, but many things can be easily handled to make long-term savings. Although there may be an initial cost, the savings will be repaid many times over.

- **Example**: I employed a gardener for maintenance regularly.
- After reviewing the cost, we decided to spend the money on getting the tools we needed to do the work ourselves.
- After three months, we saved the price of the tools and have continued saving since.
- The bonus being I get the added excercise as well.

By adopting minimalist principles, you can cut unnecessary expenses and focus your money on what truly matters, leading to greater financial freedom and peace of mind.

Planning for Irregular Expenses

Irregular expenses, such as annual insurance premiums, vehicle registration, or holiday spending, can throw off your budget if you're unprepared for them.

These expenses don't occur monthly but can be significant when they arise.

Here's how to plan for them:

Create a Sinking Fund: A sinking fund is a savings account that sets aside monthly money for specific irregular expenses.

For example, if your car insurance premium is $600 yearly, save $50 monthly in a sinking fund to cover it when it's due.

- **Tip**: Set up multiple sinking funds for different expenses, such as vacation savings, home maintenance, or holiday gifts.
- Label each fund clearly so you know exactly what it's for.

Automate Savings for Irregular Expenses: Just like you might automate savings for an emergency fund, you can automate contributions to sinking funds.

Set up an automatic transfer to a separate account each month to ensure you're always prepared for these expenses.

Include Irregular Expenses in Your Budget: When creating your monthly budget, divide irregular expenses into smaller, manageable amounts. This way, you won't be caught off guard when these bills are due.

- **Tip**: Track due dates for annual or semi-annual expenses, such as property taxes or insurance premiums.
- Add reminders to your calendar so you're always aware of upcoming payments.

Review Your Irregular Expenses Annually: Review your anticipated irregular expenses at the beginning of each year. Consider any new costs that may arise (such as a planned home renovation or a family vacation) and adjust your sinking funds accordingly.

- **Tip**: Keep a detailed list of all your annual or irregular expenses to ensure everything is included.

By planning ahead for irregular expenses, you can avoid financial surprises and ensure that these costs don't disrupt your budget.

Chapter Eleven

Guarding Your Wallet: Spotting Scams and Avoiding Fraud

Every dollar you have worked hard to earn deserves your protection

This is where things get a bit less obvious, and a lot more expensive if you get it wrong.

Scams, fraud, and financial manipulation don't always look like what you expect. They don't come with warning signs. Most of the time, they feel legitimate right up until the moment they're not.

You don't need to know every type of scam out there, but you do need to understand how they work. Because once you see the patterns, they become a lot easier to spot.

In this chapter, we'll look at some of the most common approaches and the behaviours behind them, so you're less likely to be caught off guard.

The scale of this problem is immense, with estimated worldwide losses of $1.02 trillion between August 2022 and August 2023. The top 3 target countries were Singapore, Switzerland, and Austria. It is estimated that only 7 percent of scams are reported to Authorities.

Even when reported, because of the international nature of most of these scams, there is little that the police can do. Also, it is worth noting that it is not just older people affected by these scams; 53% of victims are reported to be aged between 20 and 39.

This chapter is your guide to recognizing red flags, understanding the psychology of scams, and taking proactive steps to protect your hard-earned money. When it comes to your financial future, awareness isn't just power, it's your best defence.

Online Scam "Investments"

Online scam investments have become alarmingly prevalent in recent years, preying on inexperienced and seasoned investors alike. These scams often disguise themselves as legitimate opportunities, leveraging the trustworthiness of professional-looking websites, fake testimonials, and aggressive marketing tactics. Such schemes can be particularly appealing but equally devastating for beginners eager to grow their wealth.

Fraudulent trading platforms: These sites promise unusually high returns with little to no risk, often focusing on trending assets like cryptocurrency, forex, or binary options. Scammers lure victims with slick advertisements and fake success stories, sometimes even providing demo accounts to create a sense of legitimacy. However, once users deposit their money, it becomes nearly impossible to withdraw, and the platform either disappears or invents reasons to withhold funds.

The "too-good-to-be-true" investment opportunity: Another popular scam, fraudsters promise guaranteed returns or exclusive access to a lucrative market. They may claim insider knowledge or advanced algorithms that outperform traditional investments. While these promises might sound enticing, they often rely on classic pyramid or Ponzi schemes, where payouts to early participants are funded by new investors.

These schemes collapse and disappear as soon as recruitment slows, leaving most participants with significant losses.

Be Vigilant: One of the most effective ways for beginners to avoid online scams is to maintain a healthy level of scepticism. Always research the platform or investment opportunity thoroughly. Look for reviews, verify licenses with regulatory bodies, and pay close attention to red flags such as unregistered brokers, unclear terms, or unsolicited contact. Avoid investments that promise guaranteed returns, as legitimate opportunities always carry some level of risk.

Education is key: By learning the fundamentals of investing and understanding scammers' common tactics, you can develop the skills to distinguish between genuine opportunities and fraudulent schemes. If an investment opportunity sounds too good to be true, it probably is. Take your time, seek advice from trusted professionals, and prioritize your financial safety over the lure of quick profits.

Email, Cold Calling, and Phoney Offers

Scam investments aren't limited to online platforms; phone-based offers can be equally deceptive and damaging. These scams often begin with an unsolicited call from someone claiming to represent a legitimate investment firm or financial advisor. They may use high-pressure tactics, urging you to act quickly to avoid "missing out" on an exclusive opportunity.

Fraudsters are skilled at sounding professional and knowledgeable, making their pitches seem credible. Some might even provide fake credentials, company names, or official-sounding jargon to earn your trust. Be particularly wary of offers that demand an immediate decision or require you to transfer funds on the spot, these are classic hallmarks of a scam.

The "Nigerian" scam: This is one of the most infamous scams related to phone and email communications. Also known as the "advance-fee fraud," in this scheme, you might receive an email, message, or call from someone claiming to represent a wealthy individual, often a foreign prince, government official, or business tycoon.

The caller promises you a share of an enormous fortune in exchange for your help with a financial transaction, such as transferring money out of a politically unstable country. To proceed, they ask you to pay a fee upfront or provide your banking details. Of course, there is no fortune, and once you send the money or share your personal information, the scammer vanishes often at the same time emptying your bank account.

Fake E-Commerce: The scammers post items for sale on common shopping platforms, and the victims pay for items that are not delivered. These ads can appear legitimate with what appears to be company branding, website details, etc, but are entirely fraudulent.

- **Example:** I am on a Backyard Poultry Facebook Group. You would be surprised that even here there are often reports from other users who have been burnt by scammers creating professional looking adds for the sale of fertilised eggs or live chickens.

Job Scams: A job is offered as a terrific way to make some extra money with little to no effort. Often, it is reviewing hotels or restaurants, commenting on social media posts, etc.

The victim pays an initial deposit and gets some commission. They are then offered higher rewards with further investment. Then the company disappears, and they have lost their money.

Internet Love Scam: Preying on lonely men and women, the scammer sets up a phony profile. Initially, they just exchange chats and build confidence. But the end goal is always the same: Send money so they can purchase tickets to come and see you, or they need money to pay for immediate life-critical surgery for themselves or a close relative.

The stories are always heart-rending and coercive.

It's essential to recognize that legitimate investment opportunities rarely, if ever, come through cold calls or unsolicited messages.

Never share your financial details or send money to someone you've never met, no matter how convincing their story may sound.

By staying cautious, questioning every offer, and avoiding the pressure to make hasty decisions, you can protect yourself from falling victim to these common scams.

Fraudulent Billing and Phishing

There are as many types of scams as human ingenuity can dream up. Having said that, fraudsters are constantly devising new scams, and new victims are being targeted.

These two scams are losing some of their popularity but are still very costly to the victim, so you need to arm yourself against them.

Fraudulent billing scams are a tactic scammers use to steal money, often disguised as legitimate charges or invoices. These scams typically involve fake bills or requests for payment sent via email, text, or snail mail.

- **Example:** you receive a notice claiming you owe money for a subscription, utility service, or product you didn't order.
- The scammer aims to create a sense of urgency, pressuring you to pay quickly before you realize the bill is fraudulent.
- They may include official-looking logos or even your basic details to appear credible.
- Always verify the source of any unexpected bill by contacting the company directly using official contact information, not the one provided in the suspicious message.

Phishing: These scams take deception to another level by directly targeting personal and financial information.

In a phishing attempt, you might receive an email or text that appears to be from a trusted entity, such as your bank, an online retailer, or a popular investment platform. The message usually contains a link directing you to a fake website designed to look like the real one. Once there, you're prompted to enter sensitive information, like your login credentials, credit card details, or Social Security number.

Scammers then use this information for identity theft or to access your accounts.

- **Example:** over the past couple of months, I have been bombarded by messages from "Binance".
- They start by requesting I call to verify my identity, then progress to asking me to call to verify a suspicious log in.
- Then it's "I need to urgently call them as someone is asking to suspend my 2-factor authentication etc".

- How do I know it is a phishing scam? Every message has come from a different phone number.
- A quick read of the official Binance Customer portal says that they will never ever send an unsolicited Email, Phone Call or Message.
- Plus the fact that I have never had an account with Binance has a pretty big bearing on it as well.
- **Example:** Some of the most pernicious that have messaged me have pretended to be The IRS, Toll Road Authorities, or even The Police.
- Threatening me with jail or huge penalties if I do no contact them immediately.

The Super Prize: This is a variant on the Phishing Scams.

You get a pop up saying you have been selected to win a valuable prize because of blah blah blah. Or you can get this amazing deal on the latest Iphone XYZ. All you have to do is provide your details for shipping and cover a minor shipping cost for the item to be delivered to your door post haste.

Of course, this never happens and before you know it you are being hit with repeat charges for a subscription from a company that does not exist and has at best a dead end customer contact portal. This is because hidden deep in the blurb you actually signed up for a repeat subscription without realising it.

Never click links or download attachments from unsolicited messages to protect yourself from these scams. Instead, verify any requests directly to the company's official website.

Be cautious with emails that contain spelling errors, generic greetings, or urgent language asking you to "act immediately."

Using multi-factor authentication and updating your antivirus software can also provide an added layer of security, and remember, legitimate companies never ask for sensitive information via email or text, so always question unexpected requests.

This is only a snapshot. The methods change constantly, but the underlying patterns stay the same. Once you recognise those, you're far less likely to be caught out.

By taking these preventative measures, you'll be better equipped to protect your accounts and avoid becoming a victim of future scams.

Chapter Twelve

Monitoring Account Statements and Resolving Scam Charges

Reguarly checking your financial statements is like locking the doors to your financial house, protection starts with awareness.

Most people don't check their accounts until something goes wrong.

By then, it's usually harder to fix.

A quick look, done regularly, is often enough to catch issues early, before they turn into something bigger.

It's not just about staying on budget. It's about spotting mistakes, missed charges, or things that shouldn't be there at all.

In this chapter, we'll go through what to look for, how to recognise something that's off, and what to do if you find a charge that doesn't belong.

Why It's Important to Review Your Statements

Most people assume that if they haven't lost their card or shared their details, they're safe.

However, scammers are becoming increasingly sophisticated; even the most careful individuals can fall victim to fraudulent activity. Checking your statements regularly is one of the simplest ways to catch problems early.

Catch Unauthorized Transactions Early: Reviewing your bank and credit card statements allows you to spot unauthorized transactions before they get out of hand.

Fraud often starts small, just a few dollars to see if anyone notices. If it goes unchecked, those amounts can grow quickly.

- **Example**: Amy noticed a small $3.99 charge on her credit card that she didn't recognize.
- After contacting her credit card company, she discovered it was the first of several fraudulent charges, and the bank cancelled the card before the scam escalated.

Track Your Spending: Regularly reviewing your statements helps you stay on top of your spending.

By comparing your actual spending to your budget, you can identify areas where you may be overspending and make adjustments as needed.

- **Tip**: If you use a budgeting app or spreadsheet, compare your statement transactions with your budget categories to ensure the accuracy of your records.

Avoid Costly Errors: Mistakes happen, a double charge, a subscription renewal you didn't expect, or a billing error. By reviewing your monthly statements, you can catch these mistakes and dispute them before they affect your finances.

- **Tip**: Set up email or SMS alerts with your bank or credit card provider for transactions above a certain amount.
- You will then be notified immediately of any significant or suspicious charges.

Identify Patterns of Misuse: Scammers often target inactive or rarely used accounts because they assume you're not monitoring them closely. If you have multiple accounts, make sure to review all of them regularly, not just your primary one.

By reviewing your financial statements regularly, you can protect yourself from fraud, avoid unnecessary charges, and maintain better control over your finances.

How to Identify Suspicious Transactions

Sometimes, unauthorized transactions are obvious, but other times, they can be subtle and more challenging to detect.

Here are some signs of suspicious activity to watch for when reviewing your statements:

Small, Unexplained Charges: Scammers often start by making small charges to test whether the account is being monitored. These charges may be as low as a few cents or dollars and could be from unfamiliar companies or locations. If you don't recognize the charge, investigate it immediately.

- **Tip**: Even if the amount seems insignificant, don't ignore it.
- Contact your bank or credit card issuer right away to report it.

Unfamiliar Vendor Names: Sometimes fraudulent charges will appear under company names that seem legitimate but are unfamiliar to you. Cross-check unfamiliar vendor names with your purchase history to confirm the legitimate charge.

- **Example**: Sarah saw a charge for "ABC Digital" on her statement, which she didn't recognize.
- After contacting her bank, she discovered it was a fraudulent subscription service for which she had never signed up.

Duplicate Transactions: If you see the same charge twice for a purchase you made only once, there may have been a mistake or fraud. This can happen with in-person transactions (like restaurants or stores) and online payments.

- **Tip**: Keep your receipts to verify that the amounts on your statement match what you actually paid.

Out-of-State or International Charges: This is a red flag if you see charges from locations you haven't been to or from countries you've never visited. Scammers often use stolen credit card details for purchases in other states or countries, assuming you won't notice the charges.

- **Tip:** If you are going to travel it is a good idea to contact your Bank and Card Issuer to let them know your basic itinerary.
- Most banks have systems that flag unusual activity and may block your card.
- The problem is, you often don't realise until you try to use it.
- It has happened to me several times as I have traveled in my work.

By staying vigilant and recognizing the signs of suspicious transactions, you'll be able to catch fraud early and take steps to protect your accounts.

Steps to Take if You Find a Scam Charge

If you discover a fraudulent charge on your bank or credit card statement, acting quickly is essential.

Here's what to do if you suspect your account has been compromised:

Contact Your Bank or Credit Card Issuer Immediately: As soon as you notice a fraudulent charge, contact your bank or credit card company. Most banks have 24/7 customer service lines specifically for reporting fraud.

The sooner you report the issue, the sooner they can block the card or account to prevent further unauthorized transactions.

- **Tip**: When you call, have your account information and the details of the suspicious transaction ready.
- Your bank may ask for specific transaction details to investigate.

Freeze or Cancel the Affected Card: In most cases, your bank or credit card issuer will recommend freezing or canceling the card to prevent further unauthorized charges.

If the card is canceled, they will issue you a new one with a different number. Any pending fraudulent transactions will be blocked, and you won't be liable for the unauthorized charges in most cases.

- **Example**: After discovering fraudulent charges, and notifying the Bank of them, Lisa's bank immediately canceled her credit card and issued her a new one.
- The fraudulent transactions were reversed, and her account was protected from further theft.

Dispute the Charge: After reporting the fraudulent charge, file an official dispute with your bank or credit card issuer. Most banks allow you to dispute charges online, by phone, or in writing. The disputed amount will typically be credited back to your account while the bank investigates.

Check for Additional Fraud: Review your recent account activity for any additional suspicious charges once you've reported the initial fraud. Scammers sometimes make multiple transactions or test smaller amounts before making larger purchases.

If you find other questionable charges, report them immediately.

Change Your Account Passwords: If your account has been compromised, change the passwords for your online banking, credit card, and other financial accounts. Use strong, unique passwords, and consider enabling two-factor authentication (2FA) for added security.

- **Tip**: Avoid using the same password for multiple accounts, as this can make it easier for hackers to access your other accounts if one is compromised.

Monitor Your Accounts Closely: After resolving the issue, monitor your accounts closely for the next few months to ensure no additional fraud occurs. Consider signing up for alerts that notify you of suspicious activity or large transactions.

- **Example**: Mark set up account alerts after dealing with a scam charge. His bank now notifies him via SMS for charges over $100, allowing him to monitor his account activity more closely.

By acting quickly and following these steps, you can minimize the damage caused by fraudulent charges and protect your financial accounts from future scams.

Protecting Yourself from Future Scams

Once you've resolved a fraudulent charge, you must take steps to protect yourself from future scams. Here's how to enhance your financial security moving forward:

Enable Two-Factor Authentication (2FA): Two-factor authentication adds an extra layer of security to your financial accounts by requiring both a password and a secondary code (usually sent to your phone) for login. This makes it more difficult for hackers to access your accounts, even if they have your password.

Use Strong, Unique Passwords: Avoid using easily guessable passwords (like "password123") or reusing the same password for multiple accounts. Instead, create strong, unique passwords for each of your financial accounts. Use a password manager to keep track of them.

- **Tip**: A strong password should be at least 12 characters long and include a mix of uppercase and lowercase letters, numbers, and special characters. Unfortunately many banking Apps still only allow for 4 digit numerical passwords.

Set Up Account Alerts: Most banks and credit card companies offer alerts for account activity. You can set up alerts for large transactions, international charges, or login attempts.

These alerts allow you to detect unauthorized activity in real time.

- **Tip**: Customize your alerts to notify you via email or SMS whenever a transaction over a certain amount occurs or when your account is accessed from a new device.

Review Your Credit Report Regularly: Scammers may attempt to open new credit accounts in your name.

To catch this, review your credit report regularly for any unfamiliar accounts or inquiries. You're entitled to a free credit report annually from each central credit bureau (Experian, Equifax, and TransUnion).

- **Tip**: Consider placing a credit freeze or fraud alert on your credit report to prevent scammers from opening new accounts in your name.

Public Networks and HotSpots

Public Wi-Fi is convenient, but it's not safe for financial activity.

These networks are often unsecured, which means your data can be intercepted without you knowing. Some are even fake networks set up to capture information.

If you're logging into banking or making payments, use a secure connection.

A VPN can add a layer of protection, but the simplest rule is this:

If it matters, don't do it on public Wi-Fi.

Chapter Thirteen

Bankruptcy: A Fresh Start, Not a Failure

When all else fails: start again.

This is the point most people never want to reach.

Bankruptcy carries a lot of weight, failure, shame, the sense that something has gone badly wrong.

The reality is a bit different.

In most modern systems, bankruptcy exists for a reason. It's a legal way to reset when things have gone beyond what can realistically be managed.

It's not something to rush into, but it's also not something to misunderstand. Used properly, it can be the first step back to stability, not the end of the road.

Before getting into the detail, it's worth understanding what bankruptcy actually is, and what it isn't.

Understanding Bankruptcy

Simply put it is a legal process that allows individuals or entities unable to pay their debts to seek relief. Governed by federal laws, it offers various options tailored to different circumstances. The two most common forms for individuals are:

Chapter 7 Bankruptcy

The Bankruptcy Court may require the liquidation of non-exempt assets to repay creditors,

Exempt Items: It allows debtors to keep certain assets considered necessary for basic living and work needs. Exemptions vary by state, but common examples include:

Primary Residence: Most states offer a homestead exemption, which protects a portion of your home's equity. The amount varies widely; some states may cover the full equity, while others set specific limits.

Personal Property: Items like clothing, furniture, and household appliances are often protected up to a specific value.

Vehicles: You may keep a car, but the exemption typically applies to a specific amount of equity. If the car's value exceeds the exemption, you may need to pay the difference or surrender the vehicle.

Tools of the Trade: Essential items needed for your profession, such as tools, equipment, or a computer, are often exempt to allow you to continue earning an income.

Retirement Accounts: Most retirement savings, such as 401(k) plans and IRAs, are fully protected under federal law, though some types of accounts may have caps.

Public Benefits and Personal Income: Government benefits like Social Security, disability payments, and unemployment benefits are usually exempt, as are wages up to a certain threshold.

Exemptions are designed to ensure that filing for Chapter 7 bankruptcy doesn't leave you destitute and unable to meet your basic needs. However, anything classified as

Non-exempt Items: Luxury items, second homes, valuable collectibles, or investment properties—may be sold to satisfy creditor claims.

Understanding your state's exemption laws and working with a bankruptcy attorney is essential to fully protecting your assets and navigating the Chapter 7 process.

Chapter 13 Bankruptcy:

This is essentially a reorganisation structure to alllow the debtor time to re-structure and address their debt and creditors

Assets: Individuals can keep their assets and follow a court-approved repayment plan over three to five years.

Income: It's designed for those with a steady income who need help restructuring their debts.

Primary Residence: Your primary residence is generally protected as long as you include any overdue mortgage payments in your repayment plan and stay current on future payments.

Foreclosure: Filing for bankruptcy also temporarily halts foreclosure proceedings and gives you time to reorganize your finances. However, foreclosure may proceed if you're significantly behind on payments and the lender files a motion to lift the stay.

Consulting with a bankruptcy attorney is essential to understanding how these rules apply to your situation and the protections available for your home.

Each type has its eligibility requirements, benefits, and limitations. Consulting with a qualified bankruptcy attorney is essential to understanding which option may apply to your situation.

Bankruptcy and Taxes

Bankruptcy does not automatically cancel all tax debt, but some federal income tax debts may be discharged under certain circumstances. To determine whether your tax debts qualify for discharge in bankruptcy, they must meet specific criteria based on the type of bankruptcy filed and the nature of the debt.

Here's a breakdown:

Criteria for Discharging Tax Debt

Type of Tax Debt: Only federal income taxes are eligible for discharge. Payroll taxes, fraud penalties, and certain other types of taxes are not dischargeable.

Age of the Tax Debt: The tax debt must be at least three years old. This means the tax return associated with the debt must have been due (including extensions) at least three years before you file for bankruptcy.

Filing History: You must have filed a legitimate tax return for the debt at least two years before filing for bankruptcy. Late-filed returns may disqualify the debt from discharge.

Assessment Date: The IRS must have assessed the tax debt at least 240 days before you filed for bankruptcy.

No Fraud or Evasion: The tax debt cannot be related to fraudulent activity or deliberate tax evasion.

Chapter 7 Bankruptcy and Tax Debt: If the tax debt meets all the criteria above, it may be discharged along with other qualifying unsecured debts. However, liens placed on property before the bankruptcy filing may remain, and the IRS can still collect from the sale of those assets.

Chapter 13 Bankruptcy and Tax Debt: In Chapter 13 bankruptcy, tax debts are typically included in the repayment plan. While some debts may not be fully discharged, you can often settle outstanding taxes over the life of the repayment plan (usually three to five years) under more manageable terms. At the end of the repayment period, remaining eligible tax debts may be discharged.

Non-Dischargeable Tax Debts: Certain tax debts are not dischargeable under any bankruptcy chapter. These include:

Recent tax debts that don't meet the criteria above.

Payroll or trust fund taxes (e.g., taxes withheld from employees).

Tax liens (the lien remains on the property even if the underlying debt is discharged).

Dealing with tax debt in bankruptcy can be complex. Consulting with a bankruptcy attorney or a tax professional is critical to understanding your options and ensuring compliance with IRS and bankruptcy laws. Proper planning can maximize the relief you receive and help you navigate the process effectively.

Legal Protections and Obligations

Bankruptcy provides immediate protections under what is known as the automatic stay, which halts collection activities, including phone calls, wage garnishments, foreclosures, and lawsuits. However, it also comes with obligations:

You must fully disclose your financial situation to the court.

You may need to complete a credit counselling course before filing.

Certain debts, such as student loans, child support, and some tax obligations, may not be dischargeable.

It's a process that requires transparency and adherence to the law. Still, the legal system is designed to provide fairness to you and your creditors.

Why Bankruptcy Isn't a Shameful Choice

Financial distress can happen to anyone. Medical emergencies, unexpected job losses, or economic downturns can upend even the most carefully planned budgets. Acknowledging the need for bankruptcy is not a failure; it's recognizing your limits and a proactive step toward resolving an unsustainable situation.

In fact, some of the world's most successful individuals and companies have filed for bankruptcy and gone on to thrive. Bankruptcy allows you to wipe the slate clean and focus on rebuilding, free from the weight of insurmountable debt.

When Bankruptcy Is the Best Option

While bankruptcy is not a decision to take lightly, it can be the most responsible choice in cases where debt is overwhelming, and no other solutions exist. It allows you to regain control over your finances and your life.

Consult a qualified financial advisor or attorney to explore your options if you are considering bankruptcy. Remember, it's not about giving up, it's about starting over with the tools you need to succeed.

Rebuilding After Bankruptcy

Bankruptcy is not the end of your financial story, it's a chapter. Here's how you can start fresh after filing:

Establish a Budget: Understand your post-bankruptcy income and expenses. Stick to a strict budget that prioritizes essentials and savings.

Rebuild Your Credit: Obtain a secured credit card, pay off balances in full, and never miss a payment. Responsible credit use can gradually restore your score.

Set Realistic Goals: Focus on financial habits that promote stability, like building an emergency fund or contributing to retirement savings.

Learn From the Experience: Reflect on the circumstances that led to bankruptcy and implement safeguards to avoid repeating them.

Long-Term Ramifications of Bankruptcy

Filing for bankruptcy can provide immediate relief from overwhelming debt. Still, it also comes with long-term ramifications that require careful consideration. The most significant impact is on your **credit score**, which can drop significantly and remain affected for years. Chapter 7 bankruptcy stays on your credit report for up to 10 years, while Chapter 13 remains for 7 years.

This can make it more challenging to secure new credit, rent an apartment, or obtain favorable interest rates on loans.

Additionally, bankruptcy filings are part of the public record, which could be accessed by potential employers or lenders during background checks.

Some debts, such as student loans and child support, remain unaffected by bankruptcy, meaning you'll still need to manage those obligations.

On the other hand, bankruptcy offers the opportunity to rebuild a healthier financial foundation. By practicing responsible financial habits post-bankruptcy, many individuals are able to recover their creditworthiness within a few years and achieve greater stability.

It's important to view bankruptcy as a reset rather than an endpoint, with the understanding that rebuilding takes time, patience, and discipline.

Chapter Fourteen

Conclusion and Final Thoughts

Every financial journey starts with small steps. Stay committed and disciplined, and you will achieve the financial freedom you deserve.

By this point, you've covered a lot.

Not theory, practical changes. Where your money goes, how to control it, and how to stop it slipping away.

None of it works on its own. It works because it connects.

This chapter pulls those pieces back together, so you can see how they fit and what actually matters going forward.

Recap of Key Takeaways

Here's what it looks like in practise:

Assess Your Financial Situation: Before anything improves, you need to know where you stand. This means tracking your income, expenses, and debts and setting short-term and long-term financial goals.

Reduce Monthly Expenses: Lowering housing costs, utilities, transportation expenses, and discretionary spending can free up more money to save, invest, or pay off debt. Minor adjustments, such as meal planning and using energy-efficient appliances, can lead to significant savings over time.

Develop Financial Discipline and Mindset: Financial success is not just about numbers, it's also about developing the right mindset. Delayed gratification, staying motivated, and a positive attitude toward money will help you maintain discipline over the long term.

Build and Stick to a Budget: A personal budget is the foundation of financial success. By choosing a suitable budgeting method and regularly reviewing your expenses, you'll ensure that you live within your means and work toward your financial goals.

Save Consistently and Build an Emergency Fund: Prioritize saving by automating contributions to your savings accounts and setting up an emergency fund. A financial buffer protects you from unexpected expenses and helps you avoid debt.

Invest in Your Future: Whether saving for retirement or looking to grow your wealth, investing is key to long-term financial security. Start with affordable options, like robo-advisors, fractional shares, or low-cost ETFs, and build a diversified portfolio over time.

Monitor Your Accounts and Protect Against Fraud: Regularly reviewing your bank and credit card statements can help you catch unauthorized charges and avoid financial setbacks. Stay vigilant and take steps to protect your accounts from scammers.

Encouragement to Stick to Your Budget and Long-Term Goals

This doesn't fix itself overnight.

There will be months where it works, and months where it doesn't.

Progress Over Perfection: Don't be discouraged if you slip up or go over budget one month—what matters is that you're making consistent progress over time. Financial success isn't about perfection; it's about learning from mistakes and staying committed to your goals.

- **Tip**: If you overspend one month, don't give up. Reassess your budget, make adjustments, and keep moving forward. Focusing on what you've achieved is better than dwelling on setbacks.

Celebrate Small Wins: Every time you pay off a debt, hit a savings milestone, or make a wise financial decision, take a moment to celebrate. These small victories will keep you motivated and remind you that your efforts are paying off.

- **Tip**: Reward yourself in a way that aligns with your financial goals. For example, after paying off a credit card, treat yourself to a nice meal at home instead of splurging on something expensive.

Stay Motivated with Your "Why": When times get tough, it's important to remember why you started your financial journey. Whether your goal is to retire early, buy a home, or provide a better future for your family, keeping your "why" in mind will help you stay focused when you're tempted to stray from your budget.

- **Tip**: Write down your financial goals and keep them in a visible place, like your fridge or desk. This visual reminder will motivate you to stick to your budget and continue working toward your goals.

By staying disciplined and keeping your long-term vision in mind, you'll be able to navigate financial challenges and stay on the path to financial freedom.

Final Thoughts on Achieving Financial Peace of Mind

Financial stability isn't about having endless money.

It's about knowing what's coming in, what's going out, and not being constantly on edge about it. Whether you're paying off debt, saving for retirement, or building an emergency fund, the goal is to create a sense of stability and security in your life.

This peace of mind comes from knowing you're making wise financial decisions, living within your means, and preparing for whatever life throws your way.

As you continue your financial journey, remember that new challenges, opportunities, and changes will always exist. The economy fluctuates, personal circumstances shift, and your financial goals may evolve.

The strategies you've learned in this book are designed to give you the tools and confidence to adapt to these changes while staying on course toward your financial dreams.

Ultimately, the road to financial independence is personal.

Your journey may look different from someone else's, but as long as you stay committed to your goals, make informed decisions, and continue learning, you'll find yourself in a place of financial stability and freedom.

So, take control of your finances today. Start small, stay consistent, and believe in your ability to create a bright financial future.

You've already taken the first step, now it's time to keep moving forward.

Chapter Fifteen

Pay it Forward

When my son was three, he asked for something I couldn't afford.
I told him there was no money.
He looked at me and said, "Just get some more from the hole in the wall."

It's a simple idea, but it says a lot about how we first understand money. Unfortunately, these skills are not taught in school, and so kids need to pick them up bit by bit.

If your parents were anything like mine, money management wasn't something they were well versed in either. Basic habits, turning lights off, not wasting food, were always emphasised, probably as a hangover from Grandparents and the war years of rationing more than anything else.

In high school, economics was a core subject. I learned how to fill out a Bill of Lading and balance a Cheque Book. I was confused about why account ledgers were negative for deposits and positive for withdrawals. Fast-forward to leaving school and then starting to earn my own money, and I really had no idea. Saving for a home deposit was not something I even contemplated, and the Sharemarket was something that happened far, far away in New York on Wall Street.

As my career progressed, everything else changed with it. Technology had hit, and information was coming at us faster and faster. Banks and financial institutes changed as well. Now, instead of saving for ages to get whatever you wanted you just whacked it on the credit card. If you were about maxed out, you just requested an increase in your limit or got another card from somewhere else.

This book is the result of working through that process, step by step, and often the hard way.

The one thing I ask of you is that if, or when, you have children, you should act as the best role model and mentor you can be. The earlier kids can learn about delaying gratification, saving, allocating money for different things, and realizing that money is not a right but has to be earned, the better they will be as adults.

Various apps, such as PiggyBot, Bankaroo, and Savings Spree, are available to assist with this. And even good old Monopoly, as they get older, has its place.

As long as they understand that, they're ahead of most people. There's no such thing as a Get Out of Gaol Free card in the real world, unless you're lucky enough to have an inside track to a presidential pardon.

END

If this book helped, please take a moment to leave a short review.
Your words will help others.

References

1. **Ramsey, D. (2013).** *The Total Money Makeover: A Proven Plan for Financial Fitness.* Thomas Nelson.This book provides a step-by-step guide to financial health, focusing on debt reduction, saving, and wealth-building strategies.

2. **Siegel, J. (2019).** *Your Money and Your Life: A Lifelong Approach to Achieving Financial Freedom.* St. Martin's Griffin.A comprehensive guide that helps readers take control of their finances, set realistic goals, and develop lifelong habits for financial success.

3. **O'Leary, K. (2012).** *Cold Hard Truth on Family, Kids, and Money.* Crown B usiness.This book offers practical advice for managing finances, building wealth, and teaching financial literacy to families.

4. **Bodnar, J. (2021).** *The Debt-Free Blueprint: How to Eliminate Debt and Build Wealth on Any Income.* HarperCollins.A personal finance guide aimed at helping readers eliminate debt and make sound financial decisions to build long-term wealth.

5. **Sethi, R. (2019).** *I Will Teach You to Be Rich.* Workman Publishing.A personal finance classic, this book outlines a straightforward, no-frills plan to automate savings, budgeting, and investing.

6. **Chatzky, J. (2017).** *AgeProof: Living Longer Without Running Out of Money or Breaking a Hip.* Grand Central Life & Style.Chatzky's book tackles both financial and physical well-being, helping readers plan for the future while staying healthy.

7. **Kiyosaki, R. (2017).** *Rich Dad Poor Dad: What the Rich Teach Their Kids*

About Money That the Poor and Middle Class Do Not! Plata Publishing.A well-known book that compares two different approaches to money management, offering lessons in building wealth and financial literacy.

8. **Orman, S. (2018).** *Women & Money: Be Strong, Be Smart, Be Secure.* Random House.Suze Orman offers financial advice tailored specifically for women, helping them take control of their financial futures.

These references provide a solid foundation for understanding personal finance and budgeting. You can explore them to gain deeper insights into managing your money and achieving financial independence.

Appendix 1

Here's a step-by-step guide to creating a personal budget planner and tracker in Excel. This layout includes income tracking, expense categorization, and a summary for monthly and yearly overviews.

Step 1: Set Up Your Excel Workbook

1. Open Excel and create a new workbook.

2. Rename the first worksheet to "Budget Tracker" for tracking daily expenses and income.

3. Rename a second worksheet to "Summary" to get a monthly and yearly overview of your financial status.

Step 2: Set Up the "Budget Tracker" Sheet

Step 2.1: Create the Header Row

1. In cell **A1**, type "Date."

2. In **B1**, type "Category" (for grouping expenses, like "Groceries," "Rent," "Utilities," etc.).

3. In **C1**, type "Description" (to note specifics like "Coffee" or "Electric Bill").

4. In **D1**, type "Amount."

5. In **E1**, type "Income/Expense" to indicate if the transaction was an income or expense.

6. In **F1**, type “Month” (to track monthly transactions later).

Step 2.2: Format the Table

1. Select cells **A1**

and apply bold formatting.

1. Select the entire columns **A-F** and format them as a table by choosing **Insert** > **Table**. Check "My table has headers."
2. Customize the table format to make it easy to read.

Step 2.3: Enter Sample Data

1. Enter some sample transactions to get a feel for your layout, such as:
   - **Date**: 11/01/2024
   - **Category**: Groceries
   - **Description**: Supermarket
   - **Amount**: 50
   - **Income/Expense**: Expense
   - **Month**: =TEXT(A3, "mmm-yyyy") (for this example, it would return "Nov-2024")

Step 3: Create Drop-Down Lists

1. **Category Column**:
   - List common categories in a separate worksheet or off to the side (e.g., "Groceries," "Rent," "Entertainment").
   - Select cells in the **Category** column, go to **Data** > **Data Validation** > **List** and choose your category list as the source.
2. **Income/Expense Column**:

- Follow similar steps, but set the source list as “Income” and “Expense.”

Step 4: Set Up Monthly Totals on the "Summary" Sheet

Step 4.1: Create Headers

1. In cell **A1**, type "Month."
2. In **B1**, type "Total Income."
3. In **C1**, type "Total Expenses."
4. In **D1**, type "Net Balance" (income minus expenses).

Step 4.2: Populate Monthly Totals

1. In **A2**, enter the formula to list months automatically. For example, =TEXT(DATE(2024, ROW(A2)-1, 1), "mmm-yyyy") and drag it down to generate all months of the year.
2. In **B2**, use the formula to calculate total income for the month:

excel

Copy code

=SUMIFS('Budget Tracker'!D:D, 'Budget Tracker'!E:E, "Income", 'Budget Tracker'!F:F, A2)

1. In **C2**, use a similar formula for expenses:

excel

Copy code

=SUMIFS('Budget Tracker'!D:D, 'Budget Tracker'!E:E, "Expense", 'Budget Tracker'!F:F, A2)

1. In **D2**, calculate the net balance:

excel

Copy code

```
=B2 - C2
```

1. Copy these formulas down the column for the remaining months.

Step 5: Add Conditional Formatting

1. **Conditional Formatting for Net Balance**:
   - Select the **Net Balance** column in the "Summary" sheet.
   - Go to **Home** > **Conditional Formatting** > **New Rule** > **Format only cells that contain**.
   - Set rules:
     - Format cells greater than 0 (income > expenses) with green fill.
     - Format cells less than 0 (expenses > income) with red fill.

Step 6: Add Charts for Visualization

1. Go to the **Summary** sheet.
2. Select your **Month** and **Net Balance** data and insert a line or column chart for a quick visualization of monthly net flow.
3. Create separate pie charts to visualize category-wise expenses for a specific month by filtering your "Budget Tracker" sheet by month and using a pivot table.

Step 7: Make Your Workbook User-Friendly

1. **Freeze Panes**: In both sheets, freeze the header row by selecting **View** > **Freeze Panes** > **Freeze Top Row**.
2. **Protect Sheets**: Protect sheets (optional) to prevent accidental edits by going to **Review** > **Protect Sheet** and setting a password if needed.
3. **Create a Dashboard (Optional)**: In a new sheet, create a dashboard summa-

rizing your finances with charts and key figures like total income, total expenses, and average monthly balance.

Step 8: Test and Save Your Workbook

1. Enter sample transactions to ensure formulas update correctly.

2. Save your workbook as a template to reuse monthly or annually.

This setup will give you a functional personal budget planner and tracker in Excel.

Appendix 2

Creating a personal budget planner and tracker in LibreOffice Calc involves setting up sheets, organizing columns, adding formulas for calculations, and visualizing data. Below is a step-by-step guide:

Step 1: Set up the Spreadsheet

1. **Open LibreOffice Calc** and create a new spreadsheet (File > New > Spreadsheet).
2. **Rename Sheets**:
    - Right-click on the first sheet (Sheet1), select **Rename** and rename it to Budget.
    - Add a new sheet by clicking on the + next to the sheet tabs, and rename it to Tracker.
    - Optionally, create a third sheet for Reports or Summary if you'd like an overview of your budget status.

Step 2: Set Up the Budget **Sheet**

1. **Enter Column Headers** in Row 1:
    - In cells A1, B1, C1, and D1, type:
        - **Category** (A1): Categories like Rent, Food, Transportation, etc.
        - **Monthly Budget** (B1): The planned amount for each category.

- **Actual Spent** (C1): The actual amount spent each month.
- **Difference** (D1): Calculates the difference between the budgeted and actual spent amount.

2. **Fill in Budget Categories and Amounts**:
   - In column A (below Category), list each category you want to track (e.g., Rent, Utilities, Groceries, Entertainment).
   - In column B, enter your budgeted amount for each category.
3. **Set Up Formulas**:
   - In cell D2, enter a formula to calculate the difference between the budgeted and actual amounts:

Copy code

```
=B2 - C2
```

- Copy this formula down for each row where you've entered a budget category.

Step 3: Set Up the Tracker **Sheet**

1. **Enter Column Headers** in Row 1:
   - In cells A1, B1, C1, D1, and E1, type:
     - **Date** (A1): Date of each transaction.
     - **Description** (B1): Short description of the transaction.
     - **Category** (C1): Category to match those in the Budget sheet.
     - **Amount** (D1): The amount spent.
     - **Type** (E1): For tracking purposes, use "Income" or "Expense."
2. **Enter Transactions**:
   - Enter each expense or income in its respective column, logging every trans-

action.

- For the **Type** column, enter **Expense** for any outgoing funds and **Income** for incoming funds.

3. **Calculate Monthly Totals by Category**:
   - Use the **SUMIF** function to get the total expenses for each category.
   - Example: In the Budget sheet, assume Groceries is in row 3. In cell C3 (Actual Spent), use:

mathematica

Copy code

=SUMIF(Tracker.C:C, "Groceries", Tracker.D:D)

- Repeat this formula for each category, adjusting the criteria to match the category name.

Step 4: Set Up Summary or Reports (Optional)

1. **Create Monthly Summary**:
   - In the Reports sheet, create a summary table that includes **Total Budgeted**, **Total Spent**, and **Overall Balance**.
   - Use **SUM** functions to total the amounts in the Budget sheet for **Monthly Budget** and **Actual Spent**.
   - Calculate **Overall Balance** as **Total Budgeted - Total Spent**.

2. **Visualize Data**:
   - Use charts to visualize spending by category. For example:
     - Select data in the Budget sheet, go to Insert > Chart, choose a Pie or Bar chart, and customize it as desired.

Step 5: Automate Updates (Optional)

1. **Create Drop-down Lists for Categories**:
   - In the Tracker sheet, select cells under the **Category** column.
   - Go to Data > Validity, and set a list using your budget categories as options.
2. **Set Conditional Formatting for Overspending**:
   - In the Budget sheet, select cells under **Difference** column.
   - Go to Format > Conditional Formatting, and set rules to highlight negative balances.

This will provide you with a clear and functional budget tracker that updates automatically as you log transactions in the Tracker sheet.

Thank You

Thanks for reading.

I wrote this to help you cut through confusion and build something more stable and grounded.

One Small Favor

If this book helped you, would you take a moment to leave a quick review?

It doesn't need to be long—just a sentence or two about what you found useful. Reviews help others find the book and make a real difference.

Leave a Review

Scan the QR code or click the link below:

https://authorhelp.uk?azr=B0F74HRWL4

Also Buy Resilient Life Publishing

Practical, no-nonsense guides to help you recognise manipulation, protect yourself, and take back control in a complex modern world.

Understanding Identity and Relationships

Break Free From The Identity Trap: How Identity Was Hijacked by Culture—and How to Reclaim It

by David Sayers

Modern culture pushes constant reinvention, often leaving people more confused than clear. This book explains how identity is shaped and manipulated—and how to rebuild a grounded, stable sense of self.

Break Free From Anxious Attachment: Enhance Self-Esteem, Build Confidence, and Create Secure Relationships

by David Sayers

Anxious attachment creates cycles of worry, reassurance-seeking, and emotional strain. This guide shows why it happens—and how to build confidence, stability, and healthier connections.

Personal Security and Financial Awareness

Personal Finance Essentials: How to Track Expenses, Avoid Fraud, and Build a Sustainable Financial Future

by Oliver J. Sage

Financial stability starts with knowing where your money goes. This book shows how to manage spending, avoid common traps, and build simple habits for long-term security.

Break Free From Financial Abuse: Romance Scams, Family Pressure, and Controlling Relationships

by David Sayers

Financial abuse is control through money—often hidden inside relationships or family dynamics. This book shows how it works and how to recognise it early, protect yourself, and regain independence.

Crypto Made Simple For Seniors: Large Print, Step-by-Step Bitcoin Guide to Buying, Storing, and Gifting Digital Currency Safely

by Oliver J. Sage

Crypto can feel complex and overwhelming. This guide breaks it down into clear, simple steps—showing how to buy, store, protect, and use Bitcoin safely.

Digital Life and Modern Influence

The Age of Influence: Understanding the Hidden Economy Reshaping What We Buy and Believe

by Oliver J. Sage

Influencer culture has reshaped how products are sold and ideas are formed. This book reveals the hidden systems behind it—and how they influence what you trust, buy, and believe.

Break Free From and Avoid Fear Online: Parents' and Teens' Guide to Cyberbullying, Grooming, Sextortion, Catfishing, and Predators

by David Sayers

The online world creates real risks for families and young people. This book explains the warning signs and gives clear, practical steps to stay safe and respond with confidence.

The Big Book of Scams *(upcoming)*

A comprehensive guide to modern scams, fraud tactics, and the psychological techniques used to manipulate victims—and how to recognise them before it's too late.

Health and Well-Being

Break Free From Insomnia: A CBT-I and Natural Path to Lasting, Restful Sleep
by David Sayers
Insomnia is often driven by habits and thought patterns, not just sleep itself. This book uses proven CBT-I methods and practical changes to restore natural sleep and lasting rest.

Break Free From Recurrent UTIs: Understanding Bladder Infections, Sex Triggers, Menopause, Antibiotics, and Prevention
*by David Sayers*Recurrent UTIs rarely feel random. They follow patterns—often linked to timing, triggers, and underlying changes in the body. This book explains what's actually happening, why infections return, and how to approach prevention in a way that is practical, realistic, and grounded in how these patterns develop.

Made in the USA
Coppell, TX
05 November 2026

11302980R00082